HATE EXCEL?

Learn to love the software that can transform your confidence and career

HATE EXCEL?

Learn to love the software that can transform your confidence and career

Anne Walsh

TABLE OF CONTENTS

PRAISE FOR HATE EXCEL?

I cannot say that I've ever read a book about Excel that has actually made me laugh out loud, but this book did! If you hate Excel, there is a very good chance it is because you don't know Excel or how to use it. But how do you start? How do you push past the overwhelming sense of inadequacy to do something everyone else finds simple? How do you tame this monster so that it doesn't invoke fear and inadequacy every time you hear its name mentioned?

Written in a brilliant conversational style, following a (semi-) fictional heroine through a journey of doubt and fear to competence, this book is not about how to do the technical things (like write a VLOOKUP), but rather a book on how to LEARN Excel. Packed with humour and personal anecdotes, it will keep you reading, nodding and laughing as you learn key strategies to keep yourself moving forward through your Excel journey. And who knows... maybe, just maybe, as you move paste hating Excel, you'll find that love that many of us have for this program, and even be inspired to win an Excel Oscar one day!

Ken Puls, Excel Guru

With empathy, humour, and love, Anne Walsh made me, ME, of all people, stop cowering in fear and open an Excel spreadsheet. If she can do that for someone who breaks out in a cold sweat at the mere mention of the program, imagine what she can do for you. Anne makes the impossible and daunting world of spreadsheets approachable and even downright fun. Let her be your guide.

Jennifer Louden
- Best selling author of Why Bother?

I have never felt so seen. As someone who has actively avoided Excel for as long as I can remember, and covertly managed to hide my incompetence with it as a tool, this book helped me understand it's not my fault and that the shame and embarrassment I feel is widespread. I won't lie, some of the terminology raised my heart rate a bit, but it felt a bit like exposure therapy to make my way through the chapters. Anne's passion and humour, and the storytelling narrative of this book makes it a great read...who would have thought hey?

Julie Creffield,
Innovation Director & Ideas Coach

A solid resource that introduces the Excel-reluctant to Excel without tossing you into a sea of random Excel stuff without context or purpose. This is a necessary book that prepares the reader for what Excel is and can be, and eases into the Excel-and-data mindset.

The Excel content is refreshingly minimal but accessible through links. And the irreverent tone makes the content fun and approachable.

Oz du Soleil Excel MVP,
LinkedIn Instructor and YouTube creator at Excel on Fire

INTRODUCTION

I remember when this book "landed". It was August 2022 and I was staying in the house in Kilbrittain in west Cork where my friend was housesitting. I was sitting in the kitchen, looking out the window over the bridge, watching the birds wheel and circle, and the clouds slowly thud across the sky.

The idea for this book had been going around my head for months. Then I had the weirdest sensation. I felt as though it had actually landed in my body and I knew immediately what it would be about. This book would be for all the people, particularly women I had met, who felt fearful and shamed around Excel.

I have been teaching Excel since the early 1990s and have written eight other books on it. In that time, I have seen the same ideas and issues play out. People being expected to have learned Excel somewhere even though it's not taught as a specific topic in schools or colleges (at least in the western world). People feeling shamed, fearful and frustrated about it. I have heard the same excuses and stories about Excel over and over again. I wanted to address this issue in this book. There are many many Excel-lent technical books out there but there didn't seem to be anything for people who just didn't even know where to start.

I have grown to love Excel over the years, but I do remember what it's like to be faced with something that doesn't seem to want to cooperate with you and having no sense of how to remedy it despite all the resources out there.

STRUCTURE OF THE BOOK

I love detective stories. I started with Agatha Christie when I was a teenager and over the years I have read so many of them. So, for this book I have decided to go with a detective theme.

In this book I want you to meet Spreadsheet Sheila (she's based on a composite of people I have met over the years) and was inspired by a friend of mine, Carrie Eddins (the Blondepreneur), who has a range of characters in her posts: Spiritual Sue, Narcissistic Nina, Doubting Debbie. You can find out more about Carrie at her website: https://www.theblondepreneur.com/

We are going to travel with Spreadsheet Sheila through this book who has just started in a new job in a company called Adventure Works.

She gets herself a mentor (Laura – the Excel Goddess) to guide her as she tries to solve the case of The Work Spreadsheet. I know that you may not have access to a mentor, but I'd like you to walk along with Sheila as she works to solve this problem.

Resources

The book includes lots of resources to help you on your journey. You can find them at www.HateExcel.com

At the end of each chapter, there will be some reflection questions and exercises called Something to Do/Try/Consider

Excel formulas and functions are `formatted like this`…

Excel steps through the menu are **referenced like this:**

Here is a QR code that you can use to access the resources.

1 – SHAME, THE BIG DRIVER

"Every act of conscious learning requires the willingness to suffer an injury to one's self-esteem. That is why young children before they are aware of their own self-importance, learn so easily."

– Thomas Szasz

It was an Irish summer afternoon – which meant there had already been two showers and a rainbow. I had been working as a freelance IT trainer for about two years, and

I was working in a spacious room overlooking a shopping centre for one of my biggest customers – a training company. I hadn't known the answer to an Excel question on formulas from one participant – not great if you are the trainer, and I noticed that she hadn't come back after the afternoon tea break.

I went out to the canteen to check and there she was – her back to me, a blue angora jumper that was riding up at the back to reveal her bony spine like a miniature mountain range, and she was chatting away animatedly on her phone. I was supposed to be the trainer, and yet she didn't feel it was worth leaving their cup of tea for me. I hesitated.

I felt the shame wash up over me – like a flooded water plain that had just had a deluge. It all slapped around in one big murky mess. Shame about my inadequacies as a trainer – WHY hadn't I known the answer to that question? Shame about my chunky bulging body – that was always there. It's an essential part of the modern woman's arsenal – body shame because of course she was thin and pretty, and that just made it worse. Let's face it, body shame can be thrown at anything, and it joined in the chorus that day. Shame because I didn't ask her why she hadn't come back.

Say something or not? No, I skulked back into the classroom with my happy trainer face on – "The show must go on." I went out to check later and she had left. She hadn't even bothered to complete the obligatory "happy sheets" that participants had to complete.[1]

I often think: "If meeting participants were asked to complete these after every meeting, would corporate meetings be run differently?"

Not that it made any difference – I had stopped reading them. I knew that one negative remark would simply go straight to the bone for me. The other nine positive reviews would fade and the ink of the negative one would simply come alive and writhe and taunt me like something from a Harry Potter movie. They also were important because, as a freelancer, that's how the quality of my work was measured. It only took a few negative comments for that customer to stop working with me.

I felt shame bite me like acid and I cried slobbery snot-dripping tears on the way home.

As I cried, I found two things changing – first of all, I felt anger at her behaviour, and secondly, I swore that I would not be caught out on that question again. In fact, I found myself evoking the spirit of Scarlett O'Hara in *Gone with the Wind*.

"As God is my witness, as God is my witness – I'm not going to let Excel beat me." (I don't think those were Scarlett O'Hara's exact words...)

I may also have muttered something about not letting that little bitch get the better of me either.

So that's what I did – I worked through the exercises again, several times. And when I was asked a similar question later on – yep, I nailed it. I may also have extended a mental middle digit to Blue Angora Jumper Woman.

I am telling you this story because I want you to know that, at this stage, I definitely do know Excel better. I've written books on it and done my 10,000 hours plus of training, and my freelance work is practically all repeat business and word of mouth. It wasn't always like that. I KNOW what shame feels like and I know there is a way through. As I say in class: "I want you to learn from my mistakes."

I was asked an interesting question in the course of writing this book, as to why I thought Excel was such a source of shame for so many people. I think it is because it is "assumed" to be something easy that people will some-how pick up in school or university. Then there is the bewil-derment of finding out that it is not so easy, and I observe that, women in particular, tend to internalise shame, par-ticularly around "techie" stuff.

Shame is cruel. Brené Brown's work on shame has shown how powerful it is in stopping us being our best selves,[2] and at least, based on the comments I hear in my classes (and I have been teaching Excel since 1990) , Excel seems to be one of the big shame givers in people's work-ing lives.

If I had a Euro for the number of times I have heard people talk about how they "hate Excel" and how it ter-rifies them, I'd be living in the Cayman Islands. So often there seems to be an expectation that somehow you should know Excel automatically. If you are new to Excel, it can be rather more challenging than you had been led to believe, which leads to shame because "if it is supposed to be easy, why am I finding it so hard?"

If I am honest, shame has been a big driver in my work life, working hard to make sure that I don't give anyone ammunition to humiliate me. It has dimmed but I am still aware of it lingering there sometimes.

Are you one of the Excel haters?

If you are reading this book and Excel is part of your work life, you have probably experienced shame and confusion at some stage. I have heard so many stories of people gazing at an Excel sheet in utter bewilderment and having no idea what any of those "#ref#n/a" formulas mean. Maybe you are one of them.

In fact, you might have looked around, as my friend Christine (let's call her Christine One) did on her MBA course, and watched students around her opening up an Excel sheet as part of the finance module, and felt utterly intimidated. "I had really felt I could keep up until then, but this really floored me."

Or maybe you have been like a colleague of another Christine, let's call her Christine Two, and wept as you gazed at an impenetrable green grid of words and numbers, saying, "I'll never understand this – it is too f***ing hard."

You need to know that you are not alone – a Google search for "help with Excel" will generate 2,030,000,000 results (results as per July 2024). You are not the only person looking for help with Excel.

It is in practically every office, and it is estimated that somewhere between 1.1 and 1.5 billion people use Excel and yet it is rarely taught in any serious systematic way.[3]

That is not reflected in our education system (western world). It is usually treated as an afterthought, a sub-module of a course in schools and colleges and yet somehow when people reach the workplace they are supposed to be like Neo in *The Matrix*, "I know Kung Fu", and be able to demonstrate mastery of `PivotTables,` `formulas` and `Vlookups()` with ease. If you already feel the sweat crawling down your back at the mention of those words, know you are not alone.

So many participants will tell me "We use Excel a lot in our organisation", followed apologetically by "I'm pretty much self-taught." If I am honest, that makes me smile because HOW DO YOU THINK EXCEL TRAINERS LEARN?

Ssh, don't tell anyone.

I have heard so many times from learning participants over the years: "I'm good at most things but Excel really floors me", "I'm no good at computers/sums", "It is the worst part of my job and I never know what to do when things go wrong."

According to some research,[4] 66% of office workers use Excel at least once per hour and only 48% of people have received any formal Excel training.

If that's you, start with that. It's not your fault. The chances are you haven't been taught.

We are going to see Spreadsheet Sheila at the beginning, totally bamboozled by Excel, and we are going to walk with her as she gradually but steadily gets to grips with Excel and Solves The Case. She is going to be helped by Laura, AKA The Excel Goddess (TEG) who will guide her and offer suggestions. We are also going to spend some time going through what working through an Excel plan actually looks like. Since I am a very practical woman, there will be something to Do/Try/Consider at the end of every chapter.

Starting the case

Sheila has just started a new job in a company called Adventure Works. She had been asked about her Excel skills and had confidently said "they were good". In her mind, she thought, "Huh, how hard can it be?" She is about to find out. She has just come out of a meeting with her boss, Kim. Sheila is sitting in her open office cubicle. The walls are grey and made of a rough textured material. She knows this because she has spent the last fifteen minutes looking at them. She is afraid that she will vomit if she looks at the abomination on the screen. Sorry, the work spreadsheet (known as TWS from now on). It has nearly 30,000 rows.

She knows that because her boss said it. Kim gave her a folder with six files (which you can find in the Chapter One resources) and told her to put them together to show:

1. Total Sales by Region by Month
2. Total Sales by Category
3. Total Sales by Product Name with capability to be analysed by Occupation/Gender/Marital Status
4. Ideally with charts
5. And Slicers (whatever they were)

She told her to start by

1. Creating a master file starting with the Sales file (*AdventureWorks_Sales_2024*) and begin by using a `Vlookup()` to pull in Region name from the *AdventureWorks_Territories* file using the TerritoryKey

2. Staying with the Sales file (*AdventureWorks_Sales_2024*), pull in Customer Occupation, Customer Gender and Customer Marital Status from the *AdventureWorks_Customers* file using the matching headings and a `Vlookup()`

3. Open the *AdventureWorks_Product_Subcategories* file and update it with the correct category name from the *AdventureWorks_Product_Categories* file using ProductCategoryKey and a `Vlookup()` again

4. Open the *AdventureWorks_Products* file and update it with the correct Subcategory name and Category from the *AdventureWorks_Product_Subcategories* file using the ProductSubcategoryKey

5. Then update the Sales (*AdventureWorks_Sales_2024*) file with the Category name and subcategory name from the *AdventureWorks_Products* file using the ProductKey

6. You will need to update your Sales (*AdventureWorks_Sales_2024*) file by pulling in the Product sales price and multiplying it by the Quantity. That will be using a `Vlookup()` and a multiplication formula.

7. From this master file, use `PivotTables` with a chart and slicers to show the desired outcomes

- Total Sales by Region by Month
- Total Sales by Product Name with capability to be analysed by Occupation/Gender/Marital Status
- Total Sales by Category

You can see how all this is done in the Resources (Chapter One) which you can download at www.HateExcel.com

If it is any consolation (and I know it probably isn't), it has been broken down into sections with starting files and the completed file.

I know, you can hardly contain yourself. The excitement is too much.

She knows that is what she has to do because it was in the email she got. When her boss had actually said what was required, all Sheila had heard was a high-pitched whine, as none of that meant anything to her. Her boss had told her that it was one of those spreadsheets that got passed up the chain to the national level. Now her stomach was hollow. Her mind started to spin. What if she sends in the wrong numbers, decisions are made based on them and thousands of euros are wasted. Everything points to her incompetence. She gets fired.

She sees herself ending up under a bridge, where she is living with a three-wheeled shopping trolley, being eaten by Alsatians. (The dogs, not the people). Her incompetence leads to other people being fired and they join her under the bridge, but only to throw stones at her.

She can't go home because all the people that she got fired are marching up and down outside her house with placards calling for her death. Some of them have mentioned hanging, drawing and quartering. She didn't know what that was, but after she googled it, she realised that it wasn't a peak life experience. Sheila began to think that perhaps this line of thinking was not helpful. Distraction was required.

She looks in her handbag. Ah, her favourite commodious hard-wearing orange handbag that could be found anywhere. The one that her son and husband refused to go near: "I am NOT going in there." It falls sideways and she notices the corner of a book.

She bends down and surreptitiously pulls it out. It is a detective story – what else? She looks around the office. Yes, there they all are, noses stuck to the screens. They don't fear Excel. What is wrong with her? Time to root through the handbag of many pockets. What she wouldn't give for a cigarette now. Alas, there was none.

She pulled the book out on the desk and considered if dealing with a murder case would be easier than dealing with the spreadsheet. What would the main detective do?

Right now, she needed sustenance of the most carb variety. She went down to the canteen for a cup of tea and a nice juicy chocolate muffin, and spent ten minutes reading the book. She remembered that her heroine had a mentor/sidekick, a Watson to her Holmes, a Hastings to her Poirot.

Why was that person called a "sidekick"? Was that because you kicked them in the side? Where would she find such a person? Her muffin had disappeared but alas she knew the spreadsheet had not.

She went to queue again for a second muffin, and while she was there, she heard two people in front of her.

"Yeah, I didn't know how to do that `Vlookup()` or `PivotTable` thingy either but I asked Laura."

"You know people call her The Excel Goddess because she knows so much about Excel and she's very helpful. I asked one of the guys in IT, but he just came down and said do this and do that, and really, I was no better off."

Spreadsheet Sheila realised that she needed to meet this woman. She said, "Excuse me, who is this Excel Goddess?" They pointed across the canteen to a friendly looking woman in a navy trouser business suit. Sheila had always secretly thought that all Excel nerds wore khakis and T-shirts and were men, young men. Some of them had man buns and ponytails. Shudder.

Sheila walked over and tapped her on the shoulder. No guts, no glory.

"I hear you are an Excel Goddess and right now I need a miracle. Can you help me?"

Laura smiled and said:

"As it happens, part of my development work in the company is helping people with Excel, and I have just finished up with my current mentee so I have an open slot. Would you like to take it? Let's set up a meeting to talk. Sounds like you got your miracle. Look me up on the organisation contact list and send me an email."

Sheila walked back to her desk feeling a bit stunned. The miracle had come. The spare spot under the bridge would remain blank for a while. She looked Laura up on the company email list and contacted her. She had found her Sherlock Holmes.

Laura replied promptly and made the following suggestions:

- Ask your boss what numbers you really need to get out of the spreadsheet.

- Get last month's spreadsheet and save a copy of it. Don't work on the original.

- Get a notebook and make a note of the following:

  - Have a look at last month's spreadsheet and click on each cell and either screenshot or write down the formulas. You don't have to do them all but you need to start recognising the terms.

  - When you come across something you don't understand, write it down.

- Find out if the previous incumbent would be willing to record themselves doing the spreadsheet and send it to you.

- Ask the IT department to send someone up to go through a `PivotTable` and `Vlookup()` with you.

- If you really wanted to challenge yourself, teach one of the topics to someone else. It is scary but you would learn a lot.

- Do this one-hour course called Quick Start Excel so that you have a handle on the basics.
- **You can get access to this course at <ins>www.HateExcel. com</ins> under the Chapter 1 resources. Use the code Hate- ExcelBook to get your discount.**

They set up a Zoom meeting for the next day.

Sheila went home feeling happy. Somehow, she would get through this. The case was ON. She could solve this. Maybe she didn't have to start scouting for the bridge she would have to live under. Maybe she wouldn't have to avoid any Alsatians – yet.

> *"After all, tomorrow is another day"*
>
> – Scarlett O'Hara in *Gone with the Wind*

Something to Do/Try/Consider

"The expert in anything was once a beginner."

– Anonymous

- There may not be a Laura in your organisation but there will be people who love and can use Excel. See if you can ask them to help/mentor you. Ask for their advice.

- Get a notebook and review YOUR work spreadsheet. Note any formulas you see.

- See if you can interview the previous job incumbent and if they will help you with the spreadsheet.

- If you have A Work Spreadsheet, see if you can answer the questions posed by Laura. You can download a checklist at www.HateExcel.com

- See if your organisation is organising or offering any courses. Many companies fund Excel training for their employees. See when the next one is running. Virtual courses have the advantage that they are usually recorded which means you can review them again if you need to.

- **Sign up for Quick Start Excel course. www.HateExcel.com (Check under Chapter One resources).**

ENDNOTES

1. "Happy sheets" is the colloquial name given to the evaluation forms participants are asked to complete after a training session.
2. Brené Brown, Shame vs Guilt   https://brenebrown.com/articles/2013/01/15/shame-v-guilt/ (Date Accessed July 2024)
3. Kelly Indah, Excel users: How many people use Excel in 2024? https://earthweb.com/excel-users/ (Date Accessed July 2024)
4. Ben Richardson, Excel Facts & Statistics https://www.acuitytrain-ing.co.uk/news-tips/new-excel-facts-statistics-2022/ (Date Accessed July 2024)

2 – VISITING THE CRIME SCENE

"Take the first step in faith. You don't have to see the whole staircase, just take the first step."

– Martin Luther King Jr.

Spreadsheet Sheila is back in her cubicle but now it feels more welcoming. She has put up some photos of her beloved dog – NOT an Alsatian. She has put up a sign that says "Yes, You Can" and has decided to make Miss Marple her detective mentor. She has a photograph and if anyone asks, she has decided to say it's her Granny.

She opens up TWS (The Work Spreadsheet) from last month in preparation for her meeting with Laura. She realises that there is so much she doesn't know but somehow it feels less daunting. She decides to think of these files as her "crime scene".

She has spoken to her boss and is now clear on what she needs to get out of the spreadsheet.

- ○ Total Sales by Region by Month
- ○ Total Sales by Category
- ○ Total Sales by Product Name with capability to be analysed by Occupation/Gender/Marital Status

- These all need to be done in a `PivotTable` with charts and slicers.

- Kim also said that she needed Sheila to save each month's spreadsheet with the name of that month and year so that she could see each month-year separately.

- Kim had given her a copy of last month's spreadsheet as a starting point so at least that was something. The final version of the file is called AdventureWorks_Sales_2024_pivot_table_ready_completed and you can view it under Chapter One resources under TWS (The Work Spreadsheet) preparation.

- **She said to do that as a File | Save As. (You can find a link that explains how to do that in the resources under chapter 2 at www.HateExcel.com)**

She had signed up for the Quick Start course and had made a point of doing two sessions a day. Each one only took five minutes and felt so doable. She also felt chuffed that she had got 100% on every quiz so far. Maybe she could do this. Maybe she wouldn't have to live under a bridge with the Alsatians. Not yet anyway.

She explains to Laura what she has done. She has talked to her boss and has written down what she needs to give her and knows what files she needs to preserve as a "crime scene". There's a tiny glimmer of hope and Sheila realises that it is not as insurmountable as she had thought. There were clues in the original file.

As she explains her situation to Laura, it comes to her that she now is starting to feel as though she has a bit more of a handle on what is required. Before, it felt as though everything was just too much, too hard but as she listens to Laura, she realises, this is hard, but it is doable.

The Quick Start course is really helping in getting a feel for how to navigate around Excel and she thinks that maybe she should try a formula in a new blank sheet.

Then it seems as though Excel has been possessed by an alien. No matter where she clicks, it just keeps on doing things. She panics and just turns off the whole computer. She knows she needs a cup of tea. Was it too early for a gin and tonic? She checks the clock. It's only 9.30 a.m. What was the point?

Here she is, having got Laura to help her and done that short course, and she still can't do a f***ing basic formula.

Fear roars in her ears. What to do in the meantime? Heart starts to race. Suppose she gets this wrong. Then what? Shame forever. It seems so hard – nothing to see, no glimmer of light. She catches Miss Marple looking at her. What would she do?

Well, a detective would have to be ingenious in how to approach things and would ask if there was any other way to do this. Maybe Laura could help, but she had already given so much time and she had a meeting with her tomorrow. Of course, she could also go back and redo one of the modules in the Quick Start course or look at one of the formula cheat sheets that Laura had given her. **(Download this under the Chapter 2 resources at www.HateExcel.com)**

She asked her boss, Kim, about doing an Excel course, and Kim recommended checking with the learning and development (L&D) department about registering for the next one. There was one coming up soon and it would be online so she could fit it into her working day. In the meantime, she still had to figure out a bit more about TWS.

Going down the dead ends – some things don't work

Sheila decides to begin by asking someone from the IT department and indeed they did send up their resident twelve-year-old. He looked at her spreadsheet and said: "Oh yeah, do a `Vlookup()` there, then a `PivotTable` and chart and add in a slicer." Which Sheila thought sounded like "Blah, blah, blah."

"How do I do that?" she asked.

He bent forward, took her mouse, and clicked on what, to Sheila, seemed to be a number of random icons on the ribbon. "Like that," he said.

"Oh yes," said her voice, but her mind said, "I am completely bamboozled." It wasn't helped by the pity she saw on his face. He obviously found it hard to understand how anyone couldn't understand this stuff, and she caught the eye roll as he left.

Yet again, the shame and fear welled up and she realised that she needed to ask someone else. At least she had the name of something to search for. She promptly googles "how to do `Vlookups`". And then remembered that Laura had said, "Always add 'in Excel' to your search, otherwise you can get all sorts of random stuff." That still wasn't helpful.

She opened up last month's spreadsheet (the one that had the answers) and looked at the various formulas. She recognised some words, but realised that overall it was still incomprehensible to her.

She checked her diary. She was due to meet Laura again tomorrow.

Zooming on

"Hm," said Laura. "Couple of things you need to know. In software troubleshooting, there is the concept of stopping the symptom and then solving the problem. For example, when you do a copy and paste across, it solves the immediate issue but a more long-term solution for you would be to learn to do the following as per the actual file.

- `Vlookups()`
- `PivotTables` and charts

"I will do this month's file for you. I will record myself doing it, but for this month you need to start getting to grips with those other functions. Then for next month, you need to be able to do the other things so that you are much faster and more competent. It is like the detective story. You can follow me around for this case, but then you need to get out there yourself."

You can download a completed version of TWS and also view Laura's videos on how she put it together under the resources at www.HateExcel.com .

You will find it under the Chapter One resources in TWS (The Work spreadsheet) preparation.

"What do I do about the demented spreadsheet? I have done the Quick Start course and that feels doable. And then I look at The Work Spreadsheet, and I feel I can't do it."

Laura said:

"That's actually natural, and hopefully by me recording the steps, you will be able to recreate them, and by combining that with the course, you can start to own this baby.

"Let me talk you through some key rules with this. Write this stuff down in your notebook, and you need to practice it. It won't just jump into your head."

"True confidence comes from competence and competence comes from practice."

– Anne Walsh

Excel works as a grid

When you look at Excel, you will see that it is made up of 16384 columns (A to ...) going across the top from left to right. Then notice the rows (numbers) on the left-hand side. There are over a million. Every cell (box) has an address, made up of column and row e.g. A4, B2.

Know how to ESC(ape)

If you click on a cell and type in =, Excel thinks you want to create a formula and will think that everything you click on after that is part of a formula. This can give you the impression that your spreadsheet has been possessed. What you need to do then is to STOP, press the ESC key (top left-hand side of your keyboard) and this will get you out of formula mode. You can then start again.

Try this: Open a blank Excel workbook and type in = into an Excel cell e.g. E4. Then click on other cells. Note they start appearing in the cell you started from. To get out of that, click on the cell you started from and press ESC. Hey presto, you are back again.

Know where the Undo key is (or Ctrl and Z)

If you make a mistake, click on Undo. Most things can be undone. Then take a deep breath and start again. The beauty of Excel is that it's not like a limb amputation, where Undo is not really an option.

You can Undo most things in Excel.

Try this: Open a blank Excel workbook. Click on E4 and type in Blue. Press the Enter key. Click underneath it in cell E5 and type in Orange. Press Enter.

Now click on Undo (or Ctrl and Z together.). Orange will disappear.

Turn it off and turn it on again

Turn it off and turn it on again works surprisingly often. That is also true in life, not turning yourself on and off again. I didn't mean THAT – but hey if it takes your mind off Excel and how much you hate it for a while, go ahead. No, just take a break, step back from the computer and come back, and often it seems to be easier.

Excel is on your side

When you rest your mouse on each of the icons on the ribbon (top of the screen) you will see a little message pop up. That tells you what it does. If you are new to Excel, do not worry if you find most of them are meaningless. They will be at this point. The key thing to note is that it will tell you what it does.

Excel has examples – lots of examples

Have a look at **File | New** – you will probably see lots of tutorials there as well.

My personal favourite is the Housecleaning Checklist – #JustSaying.

Work on the copy, not the original

If you are new to Excel and you want to work on an actual spreadsheet, then create a copy. That means the original will be unharmed.

You know, there's a reason why pilots learn to fly in a simulator and surgeons learn their craft on cadavers.

Watch for copying down. If you do a formula, you can copy that down. However, if you do the same procedure with actual data like names/phone numbers you will over-write them.

Yeah, don't do that: overwrite someone's formulas and you should start making plans to leave the country.

If you are not sure what that looks like, you will find a video showing the different ways to use the mouse in the Resources for Chapter 2 at www.HateExcel.com

If you do that, go back to the second point. Click Undo.

> Don't you wish sometimes there was
> an Undo in life? You know when you have done
> and said that stupid thing.

Set up your data

If you look at any of the files in TWS section, they are all laid out in a similar way. They follow a pattern, and this is the pattern you need to watch out for.

If you are setting up your data from scratch, you need to follow certain guidelines.

- Create your headings – they should fit in one cell and be quite granular e.g. name, surname, address 1, address 2 in separate columns.

- Make the headings bold. This tells Excel to treat them as headings.

- No blank rows or columns. Blank cells are fine e.g. if you have a column for RIP, it's generally better if it is blank.

Repeating data and consistent spelling

If you are setting up a list or a database, there will be repeating data e.g. county name. Pick a spelling for that and stick with it. You, as a human, may know that Galway, County Galway, Co. Galway are all the same place. Excel doesn't know that. If you get more experienced as a database user then you could think about creating dropdown lists but for now, just remember that as a guideline. Excel will help you. If you have typed in something already and start to type it in again, Excel will autocomplete it for you. Don't take my word for it. Go into Excel, type in Blue, then underneath it Orange. Then start typing Blue again – Excel starts to complete it for you.

No ditto in data

There's no ditto in data. When I was a child, I used to love the James Herriott books. There is a story where Helen (James Herriott's wife) prepared a bill for a farmer where he had bought the same thing again, so she wrote Do meaning Ditto (same thing again). He queried the bill saying "he hadn't bought any of those Do Dos."

Unfortunately, you can do a Do Do in Data. You do need to enter the same names and details again. Alas, make sure it's a, wait for it, Don't Don't.

If you need to enter the same customers name ten times, you may think "Why should I?" Well, Excel doesn't recognise that "ditto" is the same person again. It just thinks, like the farmer in the James Herriott story that you have someone called Ditto.

You need to enter that customer name again (spelled the same way). Every row is new to Excel. It doesn't know that this new row has any relationship to the previous row. It lives in a sort of perpetual Now.

> *"There's no ditto in data."*
>
> – Anne Walsh

Watch for these common mistakes

Copying down a formula and overwriting data instead.

Doing the formula on a calculator and then writing in the formula. Don't. Do. That.

> *"It's the equivalent of having a Ferrari and deciding to get to your destination by pushing the car. Excel can do this stuff better than any of us."*
>
> – Anne Walsh

Having lots of blank spaces in your list e.g. blank columns and rows.

In Ireland, we have a TV programme called *Room to Improve*. An architect called Dermot Bannon renovates a house. After the inevitable newly discovered problems and budget battles, his solution is invariably one that includes big windows and lots of light. Spoiler alert – the budget is always exceeded. Remember light and space are desirable if you are an architect. Not so in a spreadsheet.

Time to step back

At this point, Sheila realised she was feeling a bit over-whelmed, and she still didn't feel any closer to doing what she had to do. Laura also said that she would record the creation of the `vlookups` and `PivotTables` for the next month. Sheila watched the recording, and, by repeating it multiple times, managed to recreate what Laura had done.

Laura also suggested attempting some simple Excel experiments. You can find them under Something to Do/Try/Consider at the end of this chapter.

Sometimes you just have to circle the airport

Laura said at the next meeting:

"Look, sometimes you just have to circle the airport. Do these experiments. They are not directly related to what you need to do, but you won't get so panicky if they don't work, and learning Excel is cumulative. It all counts. Some-times you just have to get through the next phase and then look at how to improve."

To quote a song "*It's not right, but it's OK*".

At the start of the next morning...

"OK. Let's take a deep breath and begin again." And as Sheila clicked on various cells, patterns were beginning to emerge. The grid idea made sense and an email came in to say that her predecessor had agreed to record how she did the file.

Sheila's mind kept telling her that she couldn't do it/ that it was too hard. It was bad enough having to battle Excel without having to battle her own mind as well.

Something to Do/Try/Consider

"You don't have to be great to start,
but you have to start to be great."

– Zig Ziglar

Try these Excel experiments

- Open up a blank Excel workbook and do the following:
  - Identify where the column headings are (A...Z) and where the row numbers are (1...a very big number)
  - Locate the ESC key (usually top left-hand corner of keyboard)
  - Spend some time in this blank Excel workbook resting your mouse on the different icons on the Ribbon and note how they tell you what they do. Do not worry if you don't know what all the terms mean.
  - Click on **File | New** and see the variety of blank templates Excel offers you. Search for something that is of interest to you and click on **Download**.

Again, do not worry if the formulas are meaning-less to you at this point. This is just about seeing what Excel can do. Close without saving.

○ **Have a look at the file called Data set up that shows you an example of a good Excel data-base set up. You will find that in the chapter 2 resources in www.HateExcel.com**

● Set up a time for someone to walk you through the spreadsheet formulas and record it. Preferably someone who is doing work similar to yours rather than the IT department.

● See if your workplace will fund a course for you or if they are offering a course.

● Buy a book – you could buy mine: *Your Excel Survival Kit – your guide to surviving and thriving in an Excel world*. Available on Amazon, getting good reviews and they are not all from my mother.

3 – IT'S A PUZZLE, NOT A PUNISHMENT

"Curiosity will conquer fear even more than bravery will."

– James Stephens

Recap:

The first month had gone fine. The figures were OK. No one died or got hurt and the bridge and the Alsatian scenario did not feel quite as vivid, although she did tend to swerve around Alsatians (the dogs, not the people) when she met them walking home. You never know.

Sheila wants to do better for the next month. She had to submit the monthly summaries of how much revenue by regions. She remembered what she had to do every month.

- Basically link all the files together with `Vlookup()` functions
- Show the sales analysed by category, region and month using `PivotTables`

When she asked Laura how long it should take her, she said, "forty five minutes max."

Sheila said, "That's impossible."

Laura laughed and said let me introduce you to the Conscious Competence Learning Model[1]

- Unconscious Incompetence (I don't know and I don't care)
- Conscious Incompetence (I don't know, I care and it feels awful)
- Conscious Competence (I can do this but only if I concentrate really hard)
- Unconscious Competence (Yes, I can do this without thinking about it)

If you drive, think of how you learned to drive a car. Did you jump into the car, and like Jeremy Clarkson in Top Gear, go from 0 to 60mph in two seconds? If you did, you shouldn't be reading this book – you should be trying to join a Formula One team. No, I am guessing you went through fear, resistance and feelings of inadequacy. I know when I was learning to drive, I stayed in first gear (I learned to drive a manual car) for ages because the idea of taking my hand off the steering wheel to change the gear AND pressing a foot pedal seemed beyond me. This was followed by the sheer terror of taking my hand off the steering wheel to change the gear before immediately grabbing it again with an iron grip.

However, I kept going and passed my driving test the first time, much to the astonishment of my husband, who had made the mistake of trying to teach me to drive a few times, which had nearly led to a "tragic domestic incident where the police aren't looking for anyone else" and where local people would comment to interviewers: "It's very quiet around here. Nothing like that has ever happened before. They were such nice people."

I am now in the Unconsciously Competent phase where I can jump in the car, drive safely to where I want to go and not remember the journey at all.

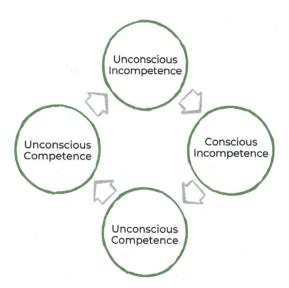

Laura said:

"You are currently in the Conscious Incompetence phase but if you keep going, hopefully next month you will be able to do this stuff slowly but competently.

"One thing you should remember is that it can take around seven to eight practice attempts to learn something. So naturally you are not good at it at this point."[2]

Sheila thought, "I'll never be as knowledgeable as that."

When she said this to Laura, she laughed and said, "You know it didn't just land in my head. I got good at Excel because I had no one to help me. I had to do particular things in my work and the IT department wasn't interested. Why would they be? Their job is to keep the whole system up and running and safe, not answer Excel problems. So I ended up asking on forums and trying to figure out stuff myself and gradually I got to grips with it. I have been where you are now. It's hard but you can progress."

> *"There's no magic. Just practise."*
>
> – Anne Walsh

Sheila knew she had to keep an open mind. After all, she always had Undo – like Paris for Rick and Elsa in the movie *Casablanca*.

What would Miss Marple do? Probably not a spreadsheet, but she would have stayed curious, kept observing and asking questions, and maybe done some experiments.

All the same, the Catastrophe Channel was beckoning, the place with the bridge and the Alsatians. She glanced down. The corner of her detective novel was visible. Well, what would a detective do?

- Get evidence to Forensics. Do some experiments. Run some tests.

- What are the patterns?

- Curate her curiosity. Start thinking about the case.

- Round up the usual suspects. Identify the most used topics.

- Revisit the scene. Begin again.

- Have a big board with what you know on it so you can step back and look.

- You need a database – unless you can remember everything. In which case, why are you reading this book?

- Stay calm and focussed. Self-soothe as required.

Get evidence to Forensics.
Do some experiments. Run some tests.

Sheila noticed that, in all the detective stories, one of the first things they did was get the evidence to Forensics and wait for the results of the post-mortem. In her case, she decided to replicate the `Vlookup()` function Laura had done on The Work Spreadsheet. She did the first one i.e. pulling in the region name into the sales file.

(You can see this done in Section One in the chapter 1 resources under The Work Spreadsheet preparation)

First time it failed, but after slowly reproducing each of the steps, it worked.

She remembered what the tutor and Laura had said: "No magic, just practice."

What are the patterns?

Remembering what the Excel Goddess had said about the patterns, she revisited the spreadsheet and looked at module 2.2 in the Quick Start course.

- Excel is a grid – identify rows/columns

- Formulas generally give answers from the same row/column and the idea is to do the formula ONCE and then copy it. This is called relative copying.

- There are exceptions. Sometimes, for example, I want to use the same VAT/tax rate with a set of numbers. So rather than typing the formula into every single cell, I put it into a separate cell and reference that cell in the formula, which you then need to "fix" by putting in dollar signs. Your "fixed" cell will look like this: A1. The quickest way to do that is by clicking on the cell and then pressing F4, or if you are using a laptop, locating a key with Fn and then pressing F4 and Fn together. You can see an example of this in section 8.5 of the Quick Start course.

- Look at the ribbon – tool tips. Sheila recognised quite a few of the icons already: B for Bold, I for Italics.

- For lists – repeating data needs to be spelled the same way all the time and needs to be kept all together.

Try this:

Open **your** Work Spreadsheet, click on a cell with formulas and check the references. Now if it has been copied down, look at the formula in the cell underneath. At this point, what are you noticing?

Curate your curiosity. Start thinking about the case.

Sheila noticed that all the great detectives had curiosity. She thought of Columbo saying "Oh, there's one other thing sir.." [3]

If you don't know who Columbo is, do a quick google for Columbo detective. Detectives like Sherlock Holmes, Miss Marple and Columbo queried why things were the way they were. For example, in the Sherlock Holmes story, *Silver Blaze*, the detective talked about "the curious case of the dog that didn't bark".

If a detective was curious, then when formulas didn't work and returned strange messages like "#Value!" the secret was to figure out what that meant rather than having a shame spiral. The error messages had meaning and they were now starting to feel intriguing rather than terrifying.

Tuning into the Catastrophe Channel murdered (ha!) her curiosity, which meant that she needed to learn to calm herself the f**k down, and work through the spreadsheet cell by cell as Laura had explained how she had done with her panicked friend Jackie. She also downloaded the list of common errors in Excel and what they meant.

(You can find them in the chapter 3 resources in the HateExcel.com website.)

Round up the usual suspects. Identify the most used topics.

The Excel Goddess had said that most Excel issues fell into a number of topics. In a detective story there were always a few people who could be in the frame for a crime, and she decided to interview the Goddess again, asking her for a list of "The Usual Suspects". I am going to call the topics that come up as the main "need to know" topics in Excel: The Usual Suspects.

Usual Suspects

1. Basic formulas: add, plus, minus, divide and how to use brackets.

2. Fix cells so they don't change location.

3. Know how to copy those formulas down and across.

4. Set up, filter and sort a list.

5. How to print.

6. How to create a chart.

7. `Vlookup()`.

8. `PivotTables` and charts.

9. Conditional formatting.

10. Work with worksheets – link formulas across worksheets and be able to manipulate worksheets e.g. create/copy/move/apply colour/hide and move/copy to another worksheet.

11. `IF functions`.

Laura said numbers 7 and 8 were needed for this spreadsheet.

How would Sheila know what to do when?

The Goddess gave her a handout called What to do when" which you can download at www.HateExcel.com (You will find it under chapter 3 resources.)

Revisit the scene. Begin again.

Spreadsheet Sheila decided to go back to TWS and try doing a `Vlookup()` by a combination of memory and referring back to her notes.

OMG, it worked! It worked, it worked. It actually f**king worked. Hands shaking, she copied down the formula. As it unfurled before her, it was a thing of beauty.

Have a big board so you can step back and see what you know already

Sheila didn't have a big board. All she had was her cubicle, notebook and maybe the table in her secret Excel hideaway. From her delightfully commodious handbag, she extracted Post-it notes, a yellow A4 pad as seen on all legal TV programmes and her big set of colouring pencils. There was a flipchart and whiteboard in the room.

She recognised that she couldn't learn everything in Excel. She had to do the equivalent of a crime scene tape and focus on what she could do.

You need a database – unless you can remember everything. In which case, why are you reading this book?

In her notebook, Sheila began to create a list of websites and resources to refer back to.

Stay calm and focussed. Self-soothe as required.

Admittedly she didn't see her detectives doing much of this. But she knew she needed to do it. She could feel the overwhelm and fear hovering at the edge of her consciousness, and she needed to find strategies that would help her self-soothe.

These are some of the strategies my participants have used.

- Remind yourself that you can do hard things. If you are an adult, you have already been through hard things.

- You have probably
  - Been a teenager.
  - Not got a job interview.
  - Had your heart broken.
  - Been bitterly disappointed by something.

- These are all hard things. You have survived them. Hell, you might even have learned something from them. There is such a thing as post-traumatic growth.[4]

- Tell yourself: "I can do this."

- Identify someone you know who has overcome hard things and think of them as your role model. Ask yourself: "What would my role model do?"

- Take deep breaths and identify the next step. Rinse and repeat. Remember you (nearly) always have Undo.

- Think of your future self who can do this stuff comfortably and competently. How good will that feel?

Sheila also notices that her mind keeps telling her that she can't do it/that it's too hard, and she begins to think that she might need to explore these stories a bit more.

This is the way for everything

Sheila tried some of the formulas again and they made complete sense.

It dawned on her that one of the greatest obstacles in this journey was her own thinking and that of the people around her who seemed to hate Excel.

Maybe the next job was to question those stories and see if there was a reframe required.

Something to Do/Try/Consider

"Progress is born of doubt and inquiry."

– Robert G. Ingersoll

- Start thinking of Excel like a puzzle and be willing to try things. After all, you (nearly) always have Undo.

- Excel is all about patterns. Can you start identifying them in your spreadsheet?

- Can you start to think about approaching Excel as a series of experiments?

- What are YOUR "Usual Suspects"? Make a list of them from your work spreadsheet.

- How would you start compiling your database of resources?

ENDNOTES

1.   Revolution Learning and Development Ltd, The Conscious Competence Learning Model, https://www.revolutionlearning.co.uk/article/conscious-competence-learning-model/ (Date Accessed July 2024)

2.   Jull Barshay, Proof Points: The myth of the quick learner, https://hechingerreport.org/proof-points-the-myth-of-the-quick-learner/ (Date Accessed July 2024)

3.   Author unknown, Columbo, negative reaction https://www.imdb.com/title/tt0071348/quotes/?item=qt0112440 (Date Accessed July 2024)

4.   Lorna Collier, Growth after trauma: Why are some people more resilient than others – and can it be taught?, https://www.apa.org/monitor/2016/11/growth-trauma, (Date Accessed July 2024)

4 – REVISIT THE SCENE

"Nothing is written"
from Lawrence of Arabia (movie) [1]

Sheila found that as she tried to get to grips with Excel, one of her biggest challenges was grappling with her own thinking. It kept getting in the way of her really leaning in and learning it. Maybe her thinking and assumptions about her own capabilities were flawed. The spreadsheet was starting to make a lot more sense and the fog was starting to clear.

Maybe her story that everyone seemed to be on top of this wasn't true, and she wasn't Idiot Island in the Competency Sea.

When she spoke to people about Excel, she kept hearing the same stories, and she began to question how true or otherwise they were. A different mindset/reframe would be so much more constructive. She could feel the fog lift as she moved from Conscious Incompetence into Conscious Competence.

Here is a quiz to help you identify your favourite story and an alternative reframe.

You can access it at www.HateExcel.com (chapter 4 resources)

Can I get me a reframe?

Maybe the stories she had been telling herself were not the whole truth. Maybe there was something else she needed to see. There had been so many stories given to her about getting to grips with Excel.

As a trainer, I have heard so many stories and excuses about Excel. I have heard them hundreds of times from Excel learners across my twenty-five years plus of Excel training. I want to call BS on them.

In the vast majority of cases in Excel, what you need to know is not a "very particular set of skills" to quote Liam Neeson in *Taken*.[2] You need to be able to do basic things, things that are well within your capabilities, which, if you are willing to learn, will save you hours of frustration. I have mentioned them before as "The Usual Suspects".

You will find the list under the Chapter Three resources in www.HateExcel.com

I have dished up my Top Ten Stories for your delectation.

- Story One – "I'm no good at technology."
- Story Two – "That's not how my mind works."
- Story Three – "I'm no good at sums/math/maths" – depending on where you are from."
- Story Four – "I'm afraid I will screw the whole thing up."
- Story Five – "I tried it before and it didn't work."
- Story Six – "I have done courses but I can't remember them."
- Story Seven – "I don't have time to learn this stuff."
- Story Eight – "We only touched on it in school/college."
- Story Nine – "I'm too young/old/tall/short/whatever excuse you are giving yourself."
- Story Ten – "This is too hard for me."

Story One – "I'm no good at tech"

Do you have a phone? Do you use Internet banking? Perhaps you have a SmartTV? You are using tech. How did you learn to use that? You are using technology all the time. You do not need to be an Excel guru but if it is part of your daily work, it will pay you to learn how to use what you need to use. You still may consider yourself no good at technology but having the equivalent of functional fitness is very empowering indeed. This will make your life much easier. For most things in Excel, it's being able to meet the equivalent of functional fitness. Can you move around unaided? Can you dress and feed yourself? That's really what is required.

Remember your Usual Suspects?

Story Two – "That's not how my mind works"

Using Excel doesn't require you to be a mathematical genius but, like all worthwhile endeavours, it takes a while to get to know and love it. If you have survived as an adult until now, the chances are you can get to grips with the basics of Excel, which is usually what you are going to need most of the time. Most of us will not be professional athletes or going to the Olympics. If you are a professional athlete or going to the Olympics, what are you doing reading an Excel book? Get out and start working on your personal best!

However, learning how to do certain basic exercises will make your life a lot easier. There is actually a World Championship for Excel[3] but you probably don't want to join that – although anything is possible! At this point identify what you do need to know and focus on that. Remember the Usual Suspects. They will cover a lot of what you need and remember that you will probably need to repeat what you do several times.

> *"Confidence comes from Competence.*
> *Competence comes from practise."*
>
> – Anne Walsh

Story Three – "I'm no good at sums/math/maths" – depending on where you are from

All the more reason to use Excel. Learn how to create your formulas once, and you can trust that your answers will be correct. I will assume that if you are reading this book, you have attended primary school. Most of the sums you need for Excel will be what you learned in primary school. You should have a ballpark figure in your head of what something should be. For example, if you are calculating someone's age and it comes out as 250 (and they are not Gandalf who is a character in Lord of The Rings [4]), you are probably wrong. For example, I was working with a learner on a `PivotTable` and it generated a set of numbers. I asked her did they look correct, and because it was her data, she knew immediately the numbers were off.

We changed a setting on the pivot table (changed the default calculation which was Sum to Count by doing a right click on the numbers and choosing Count from Summarize By in case you wanted to know) and bingo, she had her answer in minutes rather than the three hours she had planned for it, painstakingly, filtering answer by answer.

One of my favourite stories about this is a fellow Excel trainer – Claire Squibb. She says that she knew she wanted to learn how to use Excel because she wasn't good at sums. She knew that if she got the first one right, she could just copy it down/across. You just need to get the first one right. Excel will do the rest of the work.

Excel does not get tired or have to take an urgent phone call or stop to smile and chat to your annoying co-worker or have to go to the bathroom. Once you set up your formulas correctly, it will just keep going.

I have noticed that it can also work in the opposite way. One of my family members is really good at mental arithmetic and had to calculate his working hours over a year. Naturally I suggested a spreadsheet. He ignored my suggestion and instead spent days putting them all on pieces of paper and totting them up with a calculator. He spent A LOT of time on that and found himself totting up the numbers again and again. Don't do that.

Story Four – "I'm afraid I will screw the whole thing up"

That is a valid fear. Make sure you save a copy of the spreadsheet and work on the copy. There's a reason why documents are photocopied to work on or why people get a dog before having a baby.

You can do this by clicking on **File | Save As** and call it name of file – copy. Also, if you do actually screw up someone else's spreadsheet, you should google Witness Protection Programme because Death could be on the way to meet you.

Don't mess with people's lovingly tended and curated spreadsheets. Mess with the copy.

Story Five – I tried it before and it didn't work

This is one of my favourite excuses. What else have you tried that didn't work the first time? Walking? Driving? Getting married? Let's think about this.

Of course, you might not remember exactly how to do it. But this is where you need to do a favour for your future self – the future self who will be calm and confident and know how to do this and will do it in a fraction of the time, as opposed to the future self who will be going through the same pain every month because they didn't learn. The future self who – when they are asked to do something in Excel – knows what to do straight away and as a result feels gloriously competent. Eileen and Catherine, who I interviewed for this book, described how they would be completely confident in going for a job with Excel skills. As Catherine said, "I KNOW that I can do it." She was experiencing the solid confidence of competence – which comes from practice. That is, to quote a certain advertisement, priceless.[5] It also gives you solid evidence that you can do hard things, you can learn, grow and master things. What else would be possible?

If you have ambitions for promotion, having good Excel skills will only enhance that. If that is not on your radar, then think how much better it will feel to know that you can do the job competently as opposed to breaking out in a sweat every time you have to do it. Or that you need to find favours everywhere every time you need to do it. If you are in a more senior position, it doesn't help your status if you always have to ask your subordinates to do things for you. It can be really helpful if you know how to get the answer you want because then you can show them how to do it, or you can tell them which feature to use to get the answer.

Remember the Learning Cycle – you go from Unconscious Incompetence to Conscious Incompetence first.

Story Six – I have done courses but I can't remember them

Do you have a photographic or eidetic memory? Think Sheldon from *The Big Bang Theory*.[6] (If you are not familiar with *The Big Bang Theory*, it is about an incredibly clever group of physicists). Sheldon Cooper is the prodigy with the photographic memory. Do you have a photographic memory? Probably not.

So naturally, of course you can't remember everything you did.

Did you have a plan to revisit the material and practise after the course?

Probably not.

There is a thing called the Ebbinghaus effect that says you will forget approximately 50% of new information within an hour of learning it.[7] That goes up to 70% within twenty-four hours. That means YOU. Part of your learning needs to be to plan ahead for this.

If you fail to plan, plan to fail – particularly with this. The reality is that if you are not using Excel regularly, it fades quite quickly. I have been teaching Excel for years, but I know that if I am away from a topic for a few months, I have to revisit it to get it fresh in my head.

Record yourself doing the spreadsheets, add notes to it and then have that as reference material when you have to do it again. Check out Chapter 4 resources in www.HateExcel.com for tutorials on how to do that on Zoom and in Teams.

Taking notes by hand can also really help.[8]

You do have your trusty notebook nearby?

If you have learned the stuff fairly well and then return to it, it will all start coming back to you like getting stuff out of storage. There is a concept in neurology called strengthening neural pathways. The idea is that the more often you do something, the more likely you are to create neural pathways in your brain that make it easier to remember and retrieve data.[9] I have often seen people on courses who say they "haven't done Excel for a long time." But it comes back to them. As I point out on courses when I am teaching Excel, the formula to add up lots of numbers (Autosum) will not be changing any time soon.

Think of a green lawn. When you walk across that lawn once, it's barely visible. Walk across it multiple times and a path will begin to form. In fact, there is a concept in design called Desire lines.[10] The idea is that if you have a green space and let people and animals follow their own desires across it, a path will naturally form, which can be the basis of the actual path.

Story Seven – I don't have time to learn this stuff

I am guessing that you have already wasted hours on Excel – doing things manually and laboriously – maybe every month or week. That would tell me that somehow you *do* have the time to do that. I am guessing if you are reading this book, you are sick of that.

You are investing the time to learn it slowly now so that you can do it quickly and competently in the future. Then you have all that time freed up for Future You to do and learn things that really delight you. Who knows? You may learn to love and delight in Excel, but even if not, you are giving Future You a great gift. The Navy SEALs have a phrase: "Slow is Smooth, Smooth is Fast".[11] Even if you are not a Navy SEAL and have no plans to be one, that is rather Excel-lent advice.

Is the best use of your energy doing the manual stuff every month? Learning new skills is difficult. It may even feel dangerous so I am going to invoke a suggestion from one of my mentors, Jen Louden. Look around. Are there any wild animals waiting to eat you? If yes, get the hell out of there. If no, take some deep breaths, put your hand on your heart and say to yourself, "I can do this."

The beauty of the time you spend on this, learning how to do it, is that you are giving Future You a gift – the gift of the feeling of competence, of being on top of things.

You can face the difficulty now of learning this material, and as you master it, let your fear gradually fade away. Or you can put it off and let your thinking amplify its awfulness and face the time of doing it again. Excel doesn't care.

One thing that came up in all my interviews was that at some stage people chose to put time and effort into learning Excel. They chose Excel, they leaned into the difficulty and fear of it, and came out the better. This will be a decision you will need to make at some point.

Story Eight – We only touched on it in school/college

As I mentioned in chapter 1, Excel is not really taught. It's more an, wait for it, aftertaught.

It's natural that you don't know how to use it. Cut yourself some slack. You are not alone, but if you implement the learning from this book, you will be giving yourself a real head start. As they say, the best time to have learned

Excel was five years ago. The next best time is now. At least it means you have done something with it even if at the time it was hard to see its use or relevance.

Story Nine – I'm too young/old/tall/short/whatever excuse you are giving yourself

That's an excuse. If you have survived adulthood, held down a job/relationship, perhaps even parented some children, you can do Excel. After all, if you make a mistake in Excel, you can (usually) undo it. Alas, we don't have that in life. Believe you me, there are times when I could have done with an Undo button. Think of all the other situations in your life where you haven't let << Insert Favourite Excuse>> stop you doing something.

Story Ten – this is too hard for me

"I shouldn't be asked to do this. I didn't sign up for this. No one told me that I'd have to do lots of stuff with spreadsheets. I thought it was going to be all glamour, travel, meeting interesting people, dazzling people with my brilliance or baffling them with my BS," to use a quote from one of my university lecturers.

Are you thinking this? Well, unfortunately, practically every office job has Excel spreadsheets in it. You can spend the rest of your life trying to avoid them – sort of like Chandler in *Friends* who found himself on a flight to Yemen rather than have a difficult conversation with his ex-girlfriend, the nasal Janice.[12]

Alternatively, you can turn around and develop a completely different relationship with Excel.

Some ways to reframe your challenge

Problems are portals to progress – you also need to invest some of your own time

I interviewed a lot of people when I was writing this book and I noticed certain common themes. Many of them had not been taught Excel, but they found themselves running into problems and figuring out how to solve them. We are living in a time when there are many resources to learn Excel, but you will need to invest your own time to learn them.

I have included a list of some suggested ones in the Resources for Chapter 4 at www.HateExcel.com

Ken Puls,[13] who is now an MVP (basically an Excel Oscar winner) talked about how he has problems getting certain things to work in Excel and how his IT department were unable to help him. He began to do his own research about how to solve issues. He spent time figuring them out and then he found that he was answering other people's questions. This put him on the path to being one of the most respected figures in the global Excel community. Personally, I am a bit of a fangirl, but don't tell him that 🙂

Another common theme in the interviews was that they had been presented with a problem/situation and no one in their circle seemed able to solve it. So, they went off and, yes, figured it out. The beauty of this is that this approach works for many situations, not just Excel.

Perseverance is the path

"Perseverance is not a long race; it is many short races one after the other."

– Walter Elliot

All the detectives PERSEVERED. If Person A didn't help them, they asked Person B. Remember the time you invest NOW will be returned multiple times when you can comfortably and competently do the spreadsheet. This reminds me of my student Theresa. She had no spreadsheet experience, but I saw her looking in on a course with longing eyes, and I invited her to join. She did the work, solved the problems and is now the Excel Goddess in her office.

I feel a bit emotional writing about her now because she embodied everything that I talk about in this book. She admitted to me when I interviewed her for this book that she had found her job a bit boring but now is embracing Excel with a fierce enthusiasm.

"Confidence comes from competency and competency comes from practice. This is not The Matrix[14] where you sit in a chair, someone plugs you in and you know Kung Fu at the end of it."

– Anne Walsh

Something to Do/Try/Consider

> *"Be willing to be a beginner*
> *every single morning."*
>
> – Meister Eckhart

- What's your favourite Excel story?
- What would be a powerful reframe for you?
- How would your relationship to Excel change if you had a different story about it?
- What can help remind you of your new story?

ENDNOTES

1. Author unknown, Lawrence of Arabia (1962) Omar Sherif: Sherif Ali, https://www.imdb.com/title/tt0056172/characters/nm0001725 (Date Accessed July 2024)

2. Author unknown, Taken, https://www.imdb.com/title/tt0936501/ , (Date Accessed July 2024)

3. Author unknown, Microsoft Excel World Championship, https://fmworldcup.com/excel-esports/microsoft-excel-world-championship/ (Date Accessed July 2024)

4. Michael Pusey, Lord of the Rings: How old is Gandalf, https://screenrant.com/lord-rings-hobbit-gandalf-how-old-age , (Date Accessed July 2024)

5. Raja Rajamannar, Marking 25 years of Priceless, https://www.mastercard.com/news/perspectives/2022/priceless-25-year-anniversary/ (Date Accessed July 2024)

6. Author unknown, The Big Bang Theory, https://www.imdb.com/title/tt0898266/, (Date Accessed July 2024)

7.   Olivia McGarry, 5 Ways to Challenge the Forgetting Curve, https://www.learnupon.com/blog/ebbinghaus-forgetting-curve/   (Date Accessed July 2024)

8.   Fernanda Ibañez, Study reveals the Advantages of Taking Notes by hand, https://observatory.tec.mx/edu-news/study-reveals-the-advantages-of-taking-notes-by-hand/ (Date Accessed July 2024)

9.   Liz Guthridge, Want to Improve? Rewire your Brain's Neural Pathways,   https://www.forbes.com/sites/forbescoachescouncil/2024/01/23/want-to-improve-rewire-your-brains-neural-pathways/?sh=78069d9d4803 (Date Accessed July 2024)

10. Author unknown, Desire Line, https://www.merriam-webster.com/dictionary/desire%20line, (Date Accessed July 2024)

11. Author unknown, Slow is Smooth and Smooth is Fast: Navy SEALs Mantra,   https://usmilitary.com/slow-is-smooth-and-smooth-is-fast, (Date Accessed July 2024)

12. Author unknown, The One with all the Rugby, https://www.imdb.com/title/tt0583512/?ref_=fn_al_tt_1 (Date Accessed July 2024)

13. Ken Puls, Excel Guru, www.excelguru.ca, (Date Accessed July 2024)

14. Author unknown, The Matrix: Laurence Fishburne: Morpheus, https://www.imdb.com/title/tt0133093/characters/nm0000401, (Date Accessed July 2024)

5 – CLOSING IN ON THE SUSPECTS

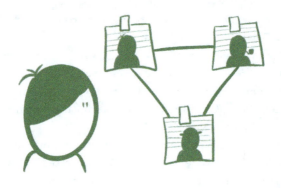

"I ain't Martin Luther King. I don't need a dream. I have a plan."

– Spike Lee

Sheila knew that at this point she had moved into the Consciously Competent phase. Thinking about going back to work again on The Work Spreadsheet left her feeling energised and excited, which she found almost unbelievable. She had asked Kim about doing more spreadsheet work, and she had been assigned some more projects. This brought home to her that she needed to tackle her Excel skill acquisition in a more systematic way. She needed a plan.

She met Laura and asked her how to proceed. "Well," Laura said, "the first thing you need to look at is how much time and bandwidth you really have for this project. You also need to assess how you operate in practice. One of the things I have found valuable is Gretchen Rubin's Four Tendencies framework.[1] And I want you to identify your Tendency."

Sheila did the quiz and discovered that she was an Obliger[2] (one of the most common types) which meant that she had to build in external accountability to ensure she stayed on track. If you find that you are a different Tendency, check out these posts from Gretchen Rubin and also her book on the Four Tendencies.[3]

Sheila also discovered a poem by Rudyard Kipling and decided to use that as her template. She thought of the detective's triad of means/motive/opportunity.

Please excuse the use of men. It's what the poem says. Rudyard Kipling won a Nobel Prize. I am not going to change his words.

I keep six honest serving-men
(They taught me all I knew);
Their names are What and Why and When
And How and Where and Who.
I send them over land and sea,
I send them east and west;
But after they have worked for me,
I give them all a rest.
From *The Elephant's Child* by Rudyard Kipling[4]

There are six main elements to the plan

- What
- Why
- When
- How
- Where
- Who

What? What I need to learn

Part of the plan was identifying what she needed to learn. For that, she reminded herself again of the Usual Suspects. But how deep did she need to go?

She asked Laura who said: "Think of this learning as a spiral. The first round will help you get a handle on the basics. Then as you go through it, you'll understand there is more to learn. Most of the time what you need to get a handle on are the basics."

You can download the Beginners Syllabus and Intermediate Syllabus at www.HateExcel.com . It is in the chapter 5 resources.

I also want to point out that while you may be a newbie to Excel you may very well need something from the intermediate syllabus. Doing the work from the beginners' syllabus will make learning the more complex stuff easier.

For example, in our story here, Sheila is a relative new-bie but she needs to know how to do more "advanced" stuff like `Vlookups()` and `PivotTables`

Why? Why do I REALLY want to learn this?

To go back to the idea of "Means, Motive and Opportunity", what is YOUR motive here? Really, honestly, why do you want to do this?

Many years ago, when I was at university, our lecturer on organisational development rather brutally commented, "When you got them by the b**ls, the hearts and minds will follow." You will feel at many times as though this journey is pointless, that it's too hard. Your favourite story will pop up with tedious regularity. This is why the previous chapter about uncovering your Excel story and offering a reframe was so important. You will need reminding of this reframe as you progress through your plan. You may have a clear Why but reinforcing the reframe will help keep you on track.

It is at this point you need to have YOUR Why clearly identified. It doesn't have to be aspirational or motivational. It has to be YOURS and this is where you need to be utterly and brutally honest with yourself.

Sheila thought about her Why. Competence and clarity were very important to her. Career progression also meant a lot, and when she checked out job requirements, nearly all of them required you to have "good Excel skills".

In some ways the reason doesn't matter, but it needs to be YOUR reason. For example, a strongly introverted family member has a goal to pay off his mortgage a bit earlier but that means if he wants to get paid more, he needs to move up a grade. In his organisation, that means he has to lead some projects, which he doesn't want to do, but the idea of being mortgage free drives him on.

Another example was Oz du Soleil (who kindly agreed to be interviewed for this book) who was puzzled by his performance stats and asked his boss for the actual data so he could analyse it.[5] He painstakingly worked through his stats filtering the data until he got what he wanted and was asked to do more Excel work. He is now an MVP and a rock star in the Excel world. Yes, I am a fangirl 🙂

For me personally, I didn't set out to be an Excel trainer. What happened was that I moved to the west of Ireland, 80km/50 miles to the nearest big city, Galway – it's really not that big a city. I had taken a year off work after the birth of our son and wanted to get back to work. Freelance training allowed me to work part time. No great plan. It was about balancing working with being a mother. My Why then was to have a life where I could combine being a mother with working.

I always say that Excel picked me. When I was asked to deliver Excel training, I said yes and found myself in situations like my opening story where I couldn't answer questions. I used my shame at this to give me fuel to make sure I could answer the questions the next time.

Knowing your true Why will keep you going when you really want to give up. It will also help grow your courage, perseverance and determination. This is just for you. No one else need see it and it may not be all that aspirational, but it needs to be YOURS. It needs to be the thing that will keep you persevering when you really want to give up. It will be the thing that will make you try one more time to get something to work. You will know if it's truly The Thing, The Big Why because you will feel it in your body. There you go: a bit of woo-woo. Bet you weren't expecting that in a book about Excel.

An exercise to help you with identifying your true Why is to keep asking yourself So What? Until you find the answer that you know is the true one.

In the list of resources for chapter 5 I have given an example of this exercise that I got from ChatGPT. www.HateExcel.com

Spreadsheet Sheila decided that her icon/inspiration for this new phase was going to be a picture of Jane Tennison (*Prime Suspect*)[6] rather than Miss Marple.

When? When will I actually do the learning?

If you want something to happen, you need to schedule it. Have a look at your diary now and identify what pockets of time/bandwidth you have to start on this project. Bear in mind this might be a moving target so it could vary from week to week. However, this might be an opportunity to start developing a practice around doing a weekly review, to reflect on your week.

There were three days a week Sheila could work on Excel, by staying in for lunch. She set aside twenty minutes, which is easily do able, and colour coded them in her calendar. Another big difference would be attending a class on Excel, registering for that went on her to-do list.

How? How am I going to learn?

Sheila finds out that they are offering an Excel course through work. It's free and done online so she signs up. She also knows that she works best when she has to actually DO the work. Unlike the character in Flann O'Brien's *The Hard Life*,[7] she comprehends that she will not be able to learn tightrope walking by correspondence course. Nor will she be able to learn Excel by watching other people.

> *"I can watch gymnastics all day long. It won't make me a gymnast."*
>
> – Anne Walsh

Believe you me, if you met me in real life, you would not confuse me with a gymnast.

Sheila knew that while instructor-led training really gets her along, she'd like to bolster it with an online course. She does some research. She asks Laura for some recommendations, and hey presto, she gives some.

You can download the list of recommended resources under chapter 5 at www.HateExcel.com

Sheila began to consider some of the courses and knew that she wanted to know the following:

- Would there be homework? (Means)
- How will she get feedback on her work? (Motive)

- She also thinks about who could help her if she gets stuck. (Opportunity)

She also thinks about what she could do in different timeslots. In ten minutes, she could learn three shortcuts. In twenty minutes, she could watch a video or do an exercise. She remembers going to a gym and the instructor talking about "exercise snacks". Maybe she could have Excel snacks.

You can download some ideas about Excel snacks under the chapter 5 resources in www.HateExcel.com

She also thinks about her story and the Ebbinghaus effect from chapter 4.[8] How was she going to retain this stuff so she could apply it? How was she going to make herself do the homework? How was she going to reward herself? She also thought about ways to make it as easy as possible for herself. She "pins" the files/folders in Excel she needs so that she has easy access. She remembered something she had seen in a newsletter about pinning the files/folders so she could access them as easily as possible.

You can view a video that shows you how to do this at www.HateExcel.com under the Chapter 5 resources.

Her Obliger tendency[9] meant that she would work better with outer accountability, which would mean working as part of a group where she had to show up.

Laura had talked about teaching others, but right now that felt a bit too scary. Maybe later on.

Where? Where am I going to learn?

Excel was on her home and work computers. What would she do if her partner or kids wanted to use it? How could she make sure she had time on it when she needed it? She had to think about this. She needed a "When Then" list e.g. when she needed to access the computer and one of the family started whinging about her "always" wanting to be on it, what would she do or say?

Who? Who can help me? I need an E-Team

She decides to create an E-Team: a list of people who can help. It includes someone from the IT department, the resident Excel goddess and the instructor on the Excel course she is doing. Books, websites and forums also can be on this list.

You can see some under Recommended Resources www.HateExcel.com (Chapter 5 resources)

What are your Training Temptations?

She also thinks about the Training Temptations: the things that could derail her efforts. For each of them she identifies how she can get around them. Here are some of the ones she came up with:

- Colleagues wanting help with something else in her review time.
- Not planning/making allowances for reviewing the materials and/or doing the homework and then realising she has forgotten it.

- Wanting to help colleagues rather than do the work.
- Putting it aside when she got stuck rather than asking for help or persevering.
- Getting stuck in an old story. She generated a list of reframes and alternatives.
- Getting the resident Goddess to do it after all.
- Not making it easy for herself to learn, to access the files.
- Her partner/kids "needing" the computer at home.
- Feeling tired/hungry and low on bandwidth.

You can do a quiz on the Training Temptations at www.HateExcel.com . You will find it under the Chapter 5 resources.

Brainstorm what possible obstacles could come up and formulate some strategies to deal with them. Identifying temptations and considering how to handle them is a strategy you can apply in a lot of areas of your life.

Rewarding your successes

Sheila knew that she wasn't very good at rewarding and reinforcing her own learning so she asked the people in her network for ideas on how to reward herself when she completed a lesson/did the homework. They all went in the notebook. This is really personal so take some time to identify what constitutes a reward for you.

- Have an ice-cream.
- Read a celebrity magazine.

- Call a friend.
- Pick flowers.
- Listen to a favourite song/playlist.
- Eat chocolate cake.
- Choose some really delightful shower gel.

Capturing the learnings

Sheila needed a way to capture her learnings. She took out her trusty notebook.

- Allow time for your brain to process the information.
- Contradiction. Visit it soon but not immediately. Your brain needs time to process it. The name of this idea is "spaced repetition".[10]
- Handwriting notes often helps.[11]
- Many people find that using mindmaps helps clarify learning as well.[12]

Something to Do/Try/Consider

> *"To achieve great things, two things are needed;*
> *a plan, and not quite enough time."*
>
> – Leonard Bernstein

- Do a first draft of YOUR plan. It doesn't have to be on a spreadsheet. Remember that it is a working document so part of this will be discovering what works for you and what doesn't.

- Identify YOUR Training Temptations and how to get around them. Your version of the "When-Then" list. Again this will be very personal.

- Come up with a list of rewards for completing an exercise.

ENDNOTES

1. Gretchen Rubin, The Four Tendencies Quiz – https: //gretchenrubin. com/quiz/the-four-tendencies-quiz/ , (Date Accessed July 2024)

2. Gretchen Rubin, How to set up accountability as an Obliger, https:// gretchenrubin.com/articles/how-to-set-up-accountability-as-an-obliger/ , (Date Accessed July 2024)

3. Gretchen Rubin, The Four Tendencies: The Indispensable Personality Profiles That Reveal how to make your life better (and other people's lives better, too), May 2018, John Murray One

4. Rudyard Kipling, 'I Keep Six Honest Serving Men' (The Elephant's Child),   https://www.kiplingsociety.co.uk/poem/poems_serving.htm, (Date Accessed July 2024)

5. Oz du Soleil, OzduSoleil, https://ozdusoleil.com/ , (Date Accessed July 2024)

6. Author unknown, Prime Suspect, https://www.imdb.com/title/ tt0098898/?ref_=fn_al_tt_1, (Date Accessed July 2024)

7. Flann O'Brien, The Hard Life, 1961, 1st edition, MacGibbon & Kee

8. Athena Marousis, What is the Ebbinghaus forgetting curve? Examples and strategies for overcoming it. https://www.talentcards.com/ blog/ebbinghaus-forgetting-curve/, (Date Accessed July 2024)

9. Gretchen Rubin, Your Tendency – Obliger, https://gretchenrubin.com/ quiz/the-four-tendencies-quiz/obliger/ , (Date Accessed July 2024)

10. Paul Martinek, Spaced repetition, https://www.khanacademy. org/science/learn-to-learn/x141050afa14cfed3:learn-to-learn/ x141050afa14cfed3:spaced-repetition/a/l2l-spaced-repetition , (Date Accessed July 2024)

11. Charlotte Hu, Why writing by hand is better for memory and learning, https://www.scientificamerican.com/article/why-writing-by-hand-is-better-for-memory-and-learning/ Accessed August 2024?

12. @Mindmaps.com, Mindmaps.com The ultimate guide to mind mapping, https://www.mindmaps.com, (Date Accessed July 2024)

6 – WORKING THROUGH THE PLAN

"One learns from books and example only that certain things can be done. Actual learning requires that you do those things."

– Frank Herbert

At this point Sheila has worked through the One Hour Quick Start programme

(you can find the link to this course under chapter 1 resources at www.HateExcel.com) so she feels comfortable enough navigating around Excel. She feels ready to move up a bit. The tutor has suggested that she use some sample files with instructions to practise on as well.

You can download the files (Practice Files) under the Chapter 6 resources at www.HateExcel.com

One of the things that always used to annoy her about movies/TV was how there would be a big kerfuffle about the plan followed by a fast forward showing you people doing fun stuff e.g. looking at a big wall board with lots of pinned photos and red thread linking them together. Or like Rocky: lots of gym work culminating in a run up a set of steps. You know, showing the end result without letting you know how much hard work was actually involved.

In this chapter I want to talk about what working through a real learning plan would look like. Books and movies gloss over this stage, and we can end up secretly thinking that there is something wrong with us because we don't find it easy.

One of my favourite stories about this is in *Singing in the Rain* where a scene that took five minutes on screen took all day and forty takes to actually do.[1] I don't want to do that here. I want to explore some of the obstacles, successes and learnings that can happen as we work through the plan.

Starting the plan – Week 1 – Monday

Sheila has decided to both do the instructor-led course offered at work and to work through the files the instructor offered as homework. There is a weekly class on Tuesday mornings she has signed up for. It is recorded so she knows she can go back and review as required.

She has looked through her diary and seen that she can do about twenty to twenty-five minutes at lunchtime on Monday/Wednesday/Thursday. She's written the slots into her calendar.

- Story reframes are written up and ready in her notebook for when the Catastrophe Channel starts playing.
- Positive self-talk phrases printed up and ready to go.
- The When-Then list for when things went wrong

She is READY and has decided where she is going to learn and what her Big Why is: to achieve that feeling of cool calm competence that oozes from Jane Tennison of *Prime Suspect*.

She also thinks it would be fun to think again about "Means, Motive and Opportunity" and how it applies to her situation.

Then she thinks, "Of course I need my 'Usual Suspects' as well."

(You will find them under chapter 3 Resources at www. HateExcel.com)

- Means: having the files ready, knowing what to work on
- Motive: The Big Why. Jane Tennison
- Opportunity: When and where
- Suspects: What are the recurring topics?

She also knew that she'd have to start over and over again, so she printed out and pinned a copy of Brendan Kennelly's poem "Begin Again". You can read it here.

The plan – Week 1

The plan – Week 1

Date	What?	When?	How?	Where?	Who?	Possible obstacles	Workaround
Week 1 – Monday	Learn how to do addition/subtraction //multiplication and division	Lunchtime – 25 minutes from her online course	Use exercises with answers	At her desk	Tutor Online videos	Getting stuck on a formula	Antidote: ask the tutor
	How to "fix" a cell					Not understanding a topic	Work through the examples again
	Using the 01 Formulas file						
Week 1 – Tuesday	Instructor-led class – covering formulas	11:15 to 12:45	On Zoom	In a quiet room	Instructor and some colleagues	Technical problems	Do a trial run to check audio and camera a couple of days before and/or ask IT support for help
Week 1 – Wednesday	Functions Sum/Max/Min/Average/ Count/CountA/	Lunchtime – 25 minutes from online course	Do exercises with answers from online course	At her desk	By herself	Internet problems	Using the exercise files that have the answer
	Using the 02 Functions file					Checking that her answers are correct	
Week 1 – Thursday	Lists: Setup, sorting and filtering	Lunchtime – 25 minutes from the course	Do exercises from the course	At her desk	By herself	Checking that her answers are correct	Doing again and checking the instructions
	Using 04 Lists file						

What actually happens

Week 1 – Monday

Lunchtime arrives and Sheila remembers that she didn't bring any lunch. At the canteen, there is a queue and she gets back to her desk twenty minutes later. Yikes, now she only has five minutes left to do the work she had planned. Where are the files?

It takes her six minutes to locate the files and the instructions. Her inner voice pipes up: "First day and you can't even get the files open. Your time is up already." Sheila grimaces to herself but thinks, "I'll do something for fifteen minutes anyway." And she put on a timer.

"Let's begin with formulas."

Learning from experience and working through the instructions – success. Sheila opened the file and went to the Addition tab and followed the instructions there. Sheila navigated to the tab called Multiplication in the 01 Formulas file. It's all about multiplying numbers. (I bet that came as a huge surprise to you.)

The file has instructions which she knows she doesn't need any more. She clicks in cell E5 and puts in = then she clicks on the word Quantity, types in * and then clicks on the word Price. #VALUE! appears in cell e5. Where was Undo when you needed it? Whew.

Shame flooded through Sheila again. She couldn't even do this basic thing. What was wrong with her? She heard the opening bars of her favourite "I can't do Excel" song playing on the Catastrophe Channel.

"When-Then" to the rescue. "Remember when it doesn't work, stop, close down and try again. No one will die or get injured if you make a mistake."

What would Jane Tennison do? Jane Tennison would revisit the crime scene and see what she had missed. Or in this case, read the instructions again and try again.

Deep breath. Close the file without saving. Open it again. And begin again. This time she started with Multiplication, followed the instructions and IT WORKED.

Sheila remembered the tutor had said that when you changed the numbers, the answer updated. Still in the Multiplication sheet, as a tentative experiment, she clicked in C5 and changed 52 to 100. Hey presto, the number in E5 changed from 3484 to 6700. This stuff was magic.

On to Subtraction. Follow the instructions. Wow, it worked. It really worked.

Division was next. Time to try without the instructions. Yep, entered the formula, copied it down and it worked.

One more sheet to do - the one on Fixed Cell. The F4 on her computer put her on mute. Sheila read the instructions again and noticed that they said press the Fn key and the F4 key if the F4 key on its own didn't work. Now where was that key? The timer went off which meant she really had to get back to work.

Damn. This was going to take longer than she'd thought. In her notebook, she wrote down what she had learned: how to write a formula, the operators (plus, minus, divide and multiply) she needed to use and a first run at using the F4 key – "fixing the cell". Well, she knew where to pick up the next time – find the Fn key 🙂

Week 1 – Tuesday – Instructor-led training

Sheila logged onto Zoom for the instructor-led class and found that because she had spent a bit of time grappling with the formulas, the instructions made a lot more sense. The instructor mentioned the importance of thinking about the ballpark range for your numbers. As she observed, "If you are calculating 10% of a 100 and you get 1000%, you are probably wrong." The instructor also allocated homework around the formulas. Today it definitely felt like progress and almost like fun to do the exercises with her colleagues.

Week 1 – Wednesday – Continuing the plan

- Files pinned and opened. Yes.
- Lunch ready. Yes.

From her last session, the Fixed Cell exercise was not completed. They had covered it in class but she still didn't understand it, so she asked the instructor again to explain why and when you would use it. The instructor said that it was about making sure the cell reference didn't change as you copied it down if you wanted to use the same cell over and over. She also reminded her that she might need to press the F4 and Fn key together to get the dollar signs to appear in the formula if she found that the F4 key didn't work on its own.

She tried that and, hey presto, it worked. The formulas made a lot more sense this time because she had worked through them already and had recognised that she needed to write down the symbols for add/subtract/multiply/divide in her notebook so that she would remember them. She decided to work through the exercises in the 01 Formulas file again, and this time it felt so much easier.

She saved her file and started on 02 Functions but only got `Autosum` done. Easy – a warm glow of success.

Continuing the plan – Week 1 – Thursday

Files ready and good to go. Lunch eaten and Sheila is getting ready to do her twenty-five minutes on Thursday when there's an unexpected fire drill. After dutifully filing out, gathering together and moaning about the weather, everyone filed back in again and lunchtime was nearly over. Her plan was out the window. The afternoon was back-to-back meetings that she couldn't get out of.

What to do?

She looked at her calendar again and saw that she could push this to Friday, so that's what she did, and noticed her own internal resistance.

- "It's Friday. I don't want to be doing Excel on Friday."
- "I am now falling behind. It's just the first week."
- "It's too hard. It's taking too long. What's wrong with me?"

She felt her stories creep back in. "It's too hard. I can't do it. I was never any good at sums, and that reminds me, that maths teacher was a right b***h." She could hear the siren sounds of a pity party coming on. Let's face it, we all like a pity party from time to time. Or is that just me?

She looked at the picture of Jane Tennison who had overcome a lot. What would Jane have done? Drunk her bottle of gin, but then showered, dressed and gone out and solved that murder...

She decided to implement the self-talk she had written down when she was identifying her Training Temptations.

- "We are still on track."
- "We knew there would be challenges and obstacles. We have just tackled one."
- "Let's make sure we've got the celebrity magazine lined up and ready to go after this."
- "I have done more difficult things than this. I can do this."

She paused, considered and looked for another way to get what she needed. She marked it in her calendar. She felt annoyed at herself that she hadn't achieved everything she wanted to this week.

She decided to do twenty minutes on Friday. At least she'd have done something.

Continuing the plan – Week 1 – Friday

Files were pinned and ready for action and Sheila was ready to start again with Functions.

She reviewed Autosum and then followed the instructions to do the other functions.

`Max()` – find the highest value,

`Min()` – find the lowest values in a list

`Average()` – get the average value of a selection of numbers

`Count()` – count how many numbers in a selection.

`Counta()` – count how many entries (numbers and text) in a selection.

Or as I like to call it Count – Anything. Think of it as being a bit like a Labrador dog that will basically eat anything.

These functions had a pattern she could follow. She thought to herself. It's a bit like a serial killer's "signature" without the compulsion to take any trophies.

However, Sheila also noticed that one of the Training Temptations was coming up. She found that colleagues were coming up to ask her questions or stopping for a chat when she was trying to work on this. Moving to a different location when she was doing her practice would help solve that challenge, and that was going to be part of the learnings she implemented.

Review of the week

Sheila took some time to review the week and identify what had worked:

- Doing her own work with the course so that she could use the tutor for reference.

- Pinning the files and having the materials ready before she started.

- Bringing her lunch on days when she was doing this.

- Positive self-talk when things didn't go to plan and to have that list nearby

- Be willing to Undo and begin again.
- A reminder of her Big Why.

What needed to be adjusted:

- Flexibility around the plan. Some topics were going to take longer than others. She didn't know what topics they would be.
- Keep going – that was the key.
- Location was important. Somewhere she would not be interrupted and she could meet up with her accountability partner.
- More time for practice.
- Things took longer than you thought.
- Revision needed to be built in. She had heard about this strategy of "spaced repetition".[2] Work on a topic, leave it and then revisit it. Your brain has been working away on it in the meantime.
- Write down the operators for formulas. Use the notebook for questions to ask Laura.

Continuing the plan – Week 2

Sheila reviewed her plan for Week 2. At the start of the week, Sheila observed that this week she had only two lunchtime slots to work on: Monday and Thursday along with the class on Tuesday. More meetings this week. One of the temptations she had had was when colleagues approached her, she felt obliged to help them. So, this week she decided to see if she could do her work in an alternative location. Surely there was a free room somewhere she could borrow, and yes there was, with a spare computer that she could log onto.

It even had blinds she could close, so that no one would know she was in there. Sheila noticed that the act of booking the room and committing to using it made her more inclined to do the work. Could she book it for the next couple of weeks? Yep, on Mondays and Thursdays at lunchtime or early in the morning.

The plan needed to be rejigged to reflect reality so she did up the plan for Week 2.

The plan – Week 2

The plan – Week 2

Date	What?	When?	How?	Where?	Who?	Possible obstacles	Workaround
Week 2 – Monday	Continue with Functions Sum/Max/Min/Average//Count/CountA	Lunchtime – 25 minutes	Use exercises from her online course with answers	At her desk	Tutor Online videos	Not getting the same answer as the exercise Unable to log in on another computer	Ask someone from her class Have the files loaded on a storage device
Week 2 – Tuesday	Online course – charts Use 03 Charts file	11:15 to 12:45	On Zoom	In a quiet room	Instructor and some colleagues	Internet connection issues	Accessing the recording afterwards
Week 2 – Thursday	Lists – sorting and filtering Use the 04 Lists file	Lunchtime – 25 minutes	Do exercises from the course	In the booked room	Try with a colleague	Not getting the answers	Taking a note of what she did get and asking the instructor

Week 2 – Monday

This time it was functions and she had her files pinned and ready to go. They seemed to be so much easier this time around, and completing the formulas homework felt effortless – even fixing cells with the F4 and Fn key. The tutor reminded them of the Ebbinghaus effect, and Sheila completed the homework immediately after the class. Success.

Week 2 – Tuesday

Today was Chart Day. She walked through the steps and she did create a chart. She heard a sound. What was it? Oh yes, pedestals cracking and falling. All those people who she admired for having a chart? Now she was one of them. Feeling good.

Week 2 – Thursday

Lists was something she hadn't managed to get to from the previous week. It reminded Sheila that things were always going to take longer than she thought. However, this felt much easier than the formulas, and it went swimmingly.

Week 2 – Review of the week

Sheila acknowledged how much she had learned this week. She thought about what had worked for her:

- Doing the homework from the course within twenty-four hours to counteract the Ebbinghaus forgetting curve.
- Having a list of people she could ask if she couldn't get a formula to work – the E-team. They didn't have to be in her organisation.

- Moving location. She was surprised by how much more she got done when she moved to a different location to do the work.

This week had gone really well so overall a win. Jane Tennison would have been proud of her. Time to celebrate. She looked through her list of ways to celebrate – chocolate cake was definitely in order.

Week 3 – planning for the week

Sheila looked back at her previous week's learning and saw that tweaking the plan as she went along had really helped. Doing her learning in another room had made a big difference. She had her files and materials ready to go. There had been times when she felt really tired and depleted, but then she knew that it was enough to watch a video. The main thing was to do something regularly. **She remembered her list of Excel snacks (www.HateExcel.com – Chapter 5)**

This week she identified two thirty-minute slots where she could do something along with the Tuesday class, which was going to be all about the `Vlookup()`. That would be on Wednesday and Thursday, and it was going to be key in mastering TWS.

Pause for dramatic music. That's optional but do listen for it.

This function was important because it had come up over and over again in her discussions with the Goddess. Even though she had reproduced the function when she did TWS, Sheila still felt that her grasp on it wasn't solid. But Sheila noticed that she had hope. Hope that she could master it. Hope that with effort and perseverance she could set up Future Sheila for a feeling of competency and joy.

The plan – Week 3

Date	What?	When?	How?	Where?	Who?	Possible obstacles	Workaround
Week 3 – Tuesday	Online course – Learn how to do the `Vlookup()` Use the 05 `Vlookup` file	11:15 to 12:45	Work through exercises given by the instructor	Quiet Room	Instructor and some colleagues	Getting it wrong in class	Doing the homework and getting feedback
Week 3 – Wednesday	Continue with the `Vlookup()`	Lunchtime – 30 minutes	Do exercises with answers from online course	In the booked room	With a colleague	Spending time talking instead of working	Ask for a third colleague to hold them accountable
Week 3 – Thursday	Continue with the `Vlookup()`	Lunchtime – 30 minutes	Look at TWS and see if she can reproduce the formula on a copy	In the booked room	On her own	Damaging the spreadsheet The formula not working and can't see why	Make a copy Ask Laura to have a look

Week 3 – Tuesday

The instructor went through the `Vlookup()` function several times, and by the fifth iteration, Sheila found that it really was starting to make sense, but knew that she needed to apply it to TWS to make sure she understood it. Homework completed and sent on to the tutor to review. Later that day she got an email from the tutor. "Well done – all completed accurately."

Week 3 – Wednesday

Time to bring her `Vlookup()` knowledge out for a spin.

First a video from the list of resources and then a read-through of the `Vlookup()` cheat sheet that you can find under the Chapter 6 resources at www.HateExcel.com

Then she opened a copy of TWS and slowly worked through the first `Vlookup()` in that file. It worked, and as she copied down the formula, the answers unfurled in front of her. Time for a fist pump and to raise a glass to Jane Tennison. Time for a well-earned chocolate muffin.

Week 3 – Thursday

She had a meeting with Laura today as well to discuss where she was at with TWS. "I am proud to report that I can now do a `Vlookup()` and I did it on TWS."

"Right," said Laura, "next step next week is to do pivot tables, and once you have that, you should be able to do TWS on your own."

Review of the week

As Sheila reflected back on the week, she noticed that she was starting to feel good about her learning. It had been challenging at times, especially at the beginning, but getting to grips with the `Vlookup()` this week had been a revelation. It was amazing to her to look at that function and know she fully comprehended it. Time to identify the last piece of the puzzle.

Note: I am aware that many users prefer to use the `Xlookup()` function, and I have included the `Xlookup()` function in my workings on TWS, but `Vlookup()` is the function available to all versions of Excel.

The plan – Week 4

The plan – Week 4

Date	What?	When?	How?	Where?	Who?	Possible obstacles	Workaround
Week 4 – Tuesday	Online course – Learn how to do the PivotTables Use the file 06 PivotTables	11:15 to 12:45	Work through exercises given by the instructor	At home	Instructor and some colleagues	Getting it wrong in class	Doing the homework and getting feedback
Week 4 – Wednesday	Continue with the PivotTables	Lunchtime – 35 minutes	Do exercises with answers from online course	In the booked room	With a colleague	Spending time talking instead of working	Ask for a third colleague to hold them accountable
Week 4 – Thursday	Continue with the PivotTables	Lunchtime – 35 minutes	Look at TWS and see if she can reproduce the pivot table in it	In the booked room	On her own	Not getting her numbers correct	Make a copy Have the completed original nearby and check the numbers

Week four – Tuesday

Again, in this one, the instructor got the group to work through several different variations of pivot tables, and much to her surprise, Sheila found that she really understood this. She did the homework immediately afterwards and click, click, click. She KNEW she had it.

Week four – Wednesday

Time to change the plan and go straight for TWS. Time to take a deep breath, make a copy and go for it. Trembling Sheila opened the file and did the pivot table and compared it to the original example she had. It was just the same. It was no longer a mystery to her. She looked again at TWS and it dawned on her that she could do every single thing that was required. Jane Tennison gazed back at her from the walls of the cubicle.

"Jane," Sheila said, "I know how good it felt for you to put those handcuffs on the criminal and say: 'You are not obliged to say anything unless you wish to do so but anything you say may be taken down in writing and may be used in evidence.'"[3]

Week four – Thursday

Sheila peered out over the walls of her cubicle and thought how differently she felt. She had left Idiot Island and had landed on the Isle of Competency. Slowly and systematically, she opened this month's bunch of files and worked her way through the tasks. It took her thirty minutes.

Review of the week

It was time for the last meeting with Laura and smiles all round. Sheila had graduated. She had completed the task allotted, and much to the delight of her boss, Sheila had added extra features like a chart and Slicers. It now felt completely doable.

Laura said, "You know that this is an ongoing journey. You can never know enough about Excel."

Something to Do/Try/Consider

> *"Everyone's got a plan until they get hit."*
>
> – Joe Louis (boxer)

- How is your learning plan coming along?
- What has helped you stay on track, and what has shown up as an obstacle?
- How will you acknowledge and celebrate your successes?
- What were the big ahas and, maybe just as important, "Oh, s**t" moments?
- What was surprising to you about your learning?
- What have you learned about yourself working through the plan?
- What if you saw problems as portals to progress?

Please take 5 minutes to leave me a review, it helps other people to decide if they want to read the book, and I'll be eternally grateful. If you're reading on Kindle just scroll to the end of the book. If you're reading the paperback, please leave a review on Amazon.

Remember, you can get the promised downloads at www.HateExcel.com or scan the QR code.

ENDNOTES

1. Author Unknown, Singin' in the Rain – Trivia, https://m.imdb.com/title/tt0045152/trivia/?ref_=tt_ql_trv, (Date Accessed July 2024)
2. Paul Martinek, Spaced repetition, https://www.khanacademy.org/science/learn-to-learn/x141050afa14cfed3:learn-to-learn/x141050afa14cfed3:spaced-repetition/a/l2l-spaced-repetition , (Date Accessed July 2024)
3. Author unknown, Right to silence in criminal cases, https://www.citizensinformation.ie/en/justice/arrests/right-to-silence-in-criminal-cases/ , (Date Accessed July 2024)

7 – ALL IS WELL THAT ENDS WELL AND ON TO THE NEXT CASE

Six months later

Sheila closed the door behind her as she left the interview room. It amazed her that she had even gone for this job. The idea of it would have been inconceivable a year ago. It was an opportunity to both grow her skills and work from home more, two things she really wanted. It had been tough but she had comfortably finished the Excel test in the allotted time. What was even more exciting was that, when they asked her about the project management and leadership skills she didn't yet have, she had described the first day in the office looking at the Excel spreadsheet and what she had done to conquer her fears and grow her skills.

The sheer terror, the Alsatian fantasies, the detective inspiration and explained: This is how I would approach this new position.

Find a mentor and practise my skills.

Work on my stories and come up with a reframe.

Have a plan.

As she reflected over the previous months, and how she had kept working on her Excel skills, she noticed that other people were coming to her with their Excel problems. She knew how terrifying they could appear and took the time to walk people through it. If there were things she did not know, she remembered the mantra:

> *"Problems are portals to progress."*
>
> – Anne Walsh

And treated them as a learning opportunity or as Laura wryly observed "AFGO – Another F***ing Growth Opportunity."

Sheila was offered the job, and as she cleaned out her desk, she found her beloved notebook and flipped through it. She KNEW how to do all this stuff. Who would have thought it?

She questioned herself – if she could move from being terrified and alone learning Excel to being empowered and motivated, what other areas of her life could she apply this to?

Some other Excel stories

These are stories from people I interviewed for the book and/or I have worked with. In some cases, I have changed the names but most I haven't.

Oz du Soleil

Oz is an MVP (basically an Oscar winner in the Excel world) and now works full-time talking about sorting out dirty data.

Oz was working in a call centre and his supervisor was constantly giving him notes that his performance was not up to scratch, that he was not doing enough calls. He felt frustrated that other people seemed to constantly get awards and promotions. He decided to write down everything he did over a week (on paper). He then thought, huh, it would be easier to see patterns if I could put this on a computer. As he beautifully put it: "I stumbled on this thing called Excel." And he immediately saw how it could help him with his quest, so he learned to sort and filter and did some charts. He went to the president of the company with the data and was impressed with "how seriously I was taken when I showed up with data."

The hospital accountant

Catherine is an accountant who works in a hospital and who painstakingly compiled her data using a mixture of manual systems and filtering. It took her two days. When she learned to use `Vlookups()` and `PivotTables`, that went down to an hour. When she went for a new job, requiring Excel skills, this is what she said: "I no longer feel like an imposter. I am now a dab hand at `vlookups()` – even if it took me three hours of trial and error."

Christine in the hospital story

Christine had left her job and been a stay-at-home mother for a good few years. She then decided to go back into the workforce, and as part of that, she did a course that included Excel. As she said in the interview, she had originally decided to focus on Word and typing because that seemed to be of more benefit. Eventually she got a job in a public sector organisation and took over a job as a data manager. While she learned a lot from her predecessor, she knew there was more to learn. She began to do some courses with me and saw that you (nearly) always had Undo. Part of her learning was to see if she could reproduce what her predecessor had done, and as she did that, she knew her learning was on a solid footing. The turning point for her was when she went on to another course with me and found herself helping other people on the course.

"Yeah. You know, you were going through stuff. And I says, Oh my God, I actually know what Anne is on about, when you used to break us up into the breakout rooms, you know, like, I wasn't, we'll say shy, or I wasn't nervous, you know that I was able to say, well I kind of know what Anne is looking for to do so I didn't mind share my screen, because I had a handle on it."

One of the key things she said was:

"Yeah, you know, it has freed me up. I'm not constantly going over my work ensuring that it's correct."

Orla in HR – Three days. Now done in an hour.

One of my students told me how she had been spending two to three days a month on manually coding hours. When she discovered how to use the `Vlookup()`, that time went down to an hour per month. All that time saved EVERY month, not to talk about the feeling of competency and knowing that her data was accurate. Also knowing that when she would be asked an ad hoc question in future, she would know how to get the data.

Mary – Working in a records office

I had another student who used to painstakingly and manually copy the entries about one set of clients across to the next week. Again, we worked on the `Vlookup()` and now she does that work in minutes, and what's more, she knows that it is accurate.

CONCLUSION

First of all, thank you for reading all the way through. I really appreciate it. I hope that you feel differently about Excel now, that walking beside Sheila through this book has helped you to feel that you are not alone, that you can learn more than you think, and what's more, to understand that, now you have conquered this topic, there's no reason that other things you might have dismissed as being beyond you are now possible.

Learning Excel skills is like buying a dog: "It's not just for Christmas. It's for life."

ABOUT ANNE WALSH

I always said that Excel picked me. I have been teaching Excel since the mid 1990s (from Excel 5.0) and have been a Master Instructor and a Microsoft Certified Trainer. Most importantly of all, I have done more than 10,000 hours as a trainer. I have written 8 books on Excel.

What I have seen over and over again is how much suffering people experience with Excel. It is not taught and yet somehow people are expected to know it. People hold themselves back, will not try for a job or promotion that they are well qualified for because "Good Excel Skills are required". I see people spending 3 days every month on something that should take the maximum of a couple of hours because they do not have the Excel skills to do it. Time that could be better spent on something else.

As a trainer, I like to "put the fun in functions" and help learners feel free to experiment with Excel. I want it to be as they say in Ireland, "a bit of craic".

I have not always been an Excel head. My first job was in Cameroon as an accounting teacher. I had never taught before but I was 21 and knew no better. I typed up my materials on an old manual typewriter and used wax stencils to copy them. I also took up the oboe a couple of years ago and got to Grade III – however I am not available for recitals. I do not wish to be arrested for crimes against music.

ACKNOWLEDGEMENTS

First of all, I want to thank the "Magnificent Four" – "this happy few" with whom I wrote this book. Thank you, Sharon, David and Debs. You kept me going.

A huge thank you to Debs Jenkins for her Book Cohort. It was a beautifully supportive structure that has helped me bring this book from an idea to something that I really hope will help transform people's relationship with Excel.

A truly huge thank you as well to Jen Louden (www.jenniferlouden.com) who walked with me along part of this journey. Meeting you and your hubby in Galway in 2023 was one of the year's highlights for me.

Big thank you to Emer O'Leary (www.emeroleary.com) who did such a wonderful job of the illustrations.

I want to thank the people who kindly agreed to be interviewed as part of this book (in no particular order as they say on the best talent shows):

- Oz du Soleil
- Claire Squibb
- Elaine Halloran
- Laura Sheridan
- Sue Bayes

- Christine P
- Catherine Flaherty

I also want to thank my beta readers – also in no particular order. Your generosity with your time and comments was priceless.

- Jackie Clifford
- Annabel Sutton
- Ann Kelly
- Alex Hewlett
- Gill Slaven

Finally, and here's some woo-woo for you, I want to thank the book who chose me to write it. I hope I have helped some people with it.

HOW TO WORK WITH ME/ CONTACT ME

Come on over to my website and take the quiz to find where you are on your Excel journey with lots of advice and recommendations, no matter where you are in your journey. www.the-excel-lady.com

You can contact me through my website:
https://the-excel-lady.com/contact/

Connect with me on LinkedIn
https://www.linkedin.com/in/theexcellady/

Use this link to see what sort of Excel user you are.
https://bit. ly/3yzI0XH

You can check out some of my online courses here
https://the-excel-lady.newzenler.com/

If you use the code HateExcelBook at checkout, you will get a discount on my courses.
Here's my YouTube channel.
https://www.youtube.com/@TheExcelLady_Ireland

Check out my first book
Your Excel Survival Kit: Your guide to surviving and thriving in an Excel world (2nd Edition)
https://amzn.to/3TVukeG

Check out my BookBoon books here

Get and Transform data
https://bookboon.com/en/
excel-get-and-transform-data-ebook

Pivot Tables Explained - Unleash this Excel Superpower and Convert your Data to Gold
https://bookboon.com/en/pivot-tables-explained-ebook

How to create Great reports in Excel
https://bookboon.com/en/how-to-create-great-reports-in-excel-ebook

Start to End: Use Excel to Track your Finances
https://bookboon.com/en/start-to-end-use-excel-to-track-your-finances-ebook

How to create great reports in Word
https://bookboon.com/en/how-to-create-great-reports-in-word-ebook

Tables in Excel
https://bookboon.com/en/tables-in-excel-ebook

Some additional resources

Embrace the learning curve: how to get through the "I suck at this and want to quit" phase.
https://www.optimistdaily.com/2024/01/embrace-the-learning-curve-how-to-get-through-the-i-suck-at-this-and-want-to-quit-phase/?utm_source=feedly&utm_medium=rss&utm_campaign=embrace-the-learning-curve-how-to-get-through-the-i-suck-at-this-and-want-to-quit-phase

Some thoughts at the speed at which people learn:

Does Everyone Learn at the Same Rate? An Intriguing Experiment

https://www.scotthyoung.com/blog/2024/02/06/learning-rate-paper/

When is learning worth the effort?

https://www.scotthyoung.com/blog/2023/05/30/learning-cost-benefit/

How much transfer should we expect between skills?

https://www.scotthyoung.com/blog/2023/04/18/skill-transfer-explained/

MORE PRAISE FOR HATE EXCEL?

If you've ever found yourself frustrated with Excel, this book is your perfect companion. Anne Walsh, with her knowledge, charisma, and honesty, transforms the daunting task of learning Excel into an enjoyable journey. From the table of contents to the conclusion, Anne's humour shines through, making you feel at ease with each lesson.

The detective theme is a brilliant touch, immersing you into the world of Spreadsheet Sheila right from the start.

This book is not just a guide; it's a story where you can relate to the characters, with practical hints and tips woven throughout. You'll find great resources, lovely famous quotes, and plenty of basics to try out. Anne encourages you to learn from colleagues who are familiar with Excel, making the learning process collaborative and fun. With its step-by-step guide, 'Hate Excel' will undoubtedly boost your confidence and comfort in using Excel. A must-read for anyone looking to master Excel with a smile!"

Joanna Forsythe, Office Manager

This transformative book will not only sharpen your excel skills but empower the reader to approach data with a newfound confidence. Anne's no jargon, straight forward approach and actionable techniques means that readers will have the ability to provide data driven insights in no time. Most importantly about this book the examples are relevant, relatable and designed to help solve real-problems, ensuring the reader gets the most of both the book and excel. This book is more than just a technical manual - it's a game changer in terms of building the reader's skills and confidence when it comes to excel.

Richard Malone,
ICT and Digital General Manager
South East Community Health

If you hate Excel you are in the right place and plenty of good company. Most of us have to use it. But most of us haven't been taught it. What doesn't help is nerd-splaining from Alex in IT. That just raises the fears and the impostor syndrome.

We need someone to sit us down, understand the stories we tell ourselves about these little green cells and give us a simple, oh so simple, route forward. Anne, The Excel Lady, is that someone. This gem of a book is empathic, funny and downright practical. Anne understands the reluctant adult learner and I love her per-sonification of The Work Spreadsheet. We follow our hero Sheila as she battles TWS. Spoiler: she wins because she has an Anne all of her own.

With her help you will be pivoting the great green grid in next to no time, saving yourself hours in the process. But this book con-tains the roadmap to learning any new work skill, which in this ever changing world might be the ultimate lesson.

Emma Williams
- Research Career Consultant. Author of Leaving
Academia: Ditch the blanket, take the skills (2024)

I was in the middle of a difficult case, it was complex, with pages of data that I had trouble organizing, when I stumbled upon a gem—Anne Walsh's "Hate Excel." As a detective, I'm no stranger to complexity and chaos, but Excel had always been my nem-esis, a puzzle I couldn't quite solve. Until now.

Walsh speaks directly to those of us who have stared at a spread-sheet in dread, feeling as though the numbers were mocking us. She weaves her tale with the finesse of an experienced sleuth, unraveling the mysteries of Excel with a clarity that's as comforting as a warm cup of coffee on a stakeout. Her stories of Spreadsheet Sheila and the Excel Goddess bring a human touch to the cold, hard data, transforming the learning process into an engaging, almost cinematic experience.

This book is more than just a guide; it's a mentor in print. With every chapter, every resource, and every exercise, it felt like I had a seasoned expert at my side, guiding me through the twists and turns of data management. "Hate Excel" is a must-read for anyone looking to master Excel, whether you're solving crimes or just trying to keep your data in order.

Anne Walsh has crafted a beacon of knowledge in the foggy world of spreadsheets, and for that, I tip my fedora to her. The insights and practical advice contained within are invaluable, making the once-daunting task of navigating Excel not only manageable but also enjoyable. Each lesson will lead readers closer to fully comprehending Excel, making "Hate Excel" a phrase that is replaced by "Empowered by Excel."

Catherine Mondragon - Miss Resources

If Excel were a murder mystery, Anne Walsh would be the detective who solves the case with a spreadsheet instead of a magnifying glass. Her humour and storytelling make Excel less of a crime scene and more of a puzzle you actually want to solve. With Anne as your guide, even the most stubborn cells don't stand a chance!

Debbie Jenkins, Author & Publisher

Anne's supportive style in the book is a great guide for anyone new to Excel. She uses perfectly weaved in quotes along the way to break down the learning process, putting the reader at ease on their own personal journey.

Aisling Dullaghan,
Organisational Development, IDA Ireland

Having known Anne and her straightforward, engaging and witty communication style, for several years I knew this book was going to be extremely accessible for even the most scared of 'Spreadsheet Sheilas'. However this book does more than teach you how to use Excel. It takes you on a journey of self-discovery. You understand why your fear of learning something new exists, the path you need to go on to get past that fear and the kind of accountability and support you need to do it. This understanding applies to learning anything not just Excel and this knowledge and self-awareness will be worth way more than the price of this book.

Susannah Simmons,
Founder & Customer Success Specialist at ProductivIT

I thought I was pretty good at Excel. After all, I started my training career teaching it! That was too many years ago to count though, so you can imagine my utter horror when Anne Walsh's words hit home. You know, the WORDS: Vlookups ; PivotTables ; Slicers – the ones that sound so scientific and keep me awake at night, because surely these weren't A Thing when I delivered Excel training 30 years ago, and exactly when did I become a troglodyte?

Scattered with Anne's humour and references to favourite books and movies, this book will draw you into Spreadsheet Sheila's very own crime story. You'll feel her shame, her frustration and then BOOM! You will revel in her moments of discovery and triumph – because you've done the Something to Do/Try/Consider at the end of each chapter.

And in the interim, you've also worked on your mindset and tactics around learning something new that may have originally scared the sh*t out of you.

And not an Alsation in sight.

Gayle Thompson, Business Owner at VILT

In this book, Anne has created a symphony of knowledge and a step by step approach for anybody wishing to learn Excel. She makes the complex simple.

Woven into each chapter is Anne's expertise and curated resources coupled with her empathic understanding of the learners journey and what it takes to become competent and confident in developing new skills.

Her characters and their stories bring alive our own experience of failure and success when imposter syndrome or self-doubt rears its ugly head. Anne's wicked sense of humour helps put back the 'fun into function' and the human into tech.

Dolores Cummins, Director

I used to think Excel was just a boring business tool for other people. But "Hate Excel" by Anne Walsh gave me the metaphorical slap around the chops to think again. I knew Anne was a great storyteller, but the way she wove the highs and lows that led to spreadsheet serenity kept me hooked from start to finish and made me feel smarter and more capable than I ever thought possible. This book is like a cool drink on a hot day for anyone wanting to harness the practical power of Excel. To quote The Monkeys, 'I'm a believer.'

David Pullan,
Founder of The Story Spotters and
author of *The DNA of Engagement*

I have known Anne Walsh for a number of years. We met in the Trainer Talk community and I was immediately struck by both her warmth and her humour. You will find both of these in the pages of this book - alongside a veritable treasury of knowledge of Excel. This is your opportunity to learn from someone who is a daily learner herself, and someone who has the rare ability to translate complex ideas into understandable information. This book will take you on a wonderful adventure into places you didn't know were possible in a computer programme!

Jackie Clifford Director,
Clarity Learning and Development

I loved 'Hate Excel' Using the framework of 'being like a detective solving the case' Anne makes it almost a no brainer to learn the every day Excel skills needed for work.

With great humour and humanity, Anne addresses the fears, emotions and overthinking that can get in your way and gives you ways to handle them.

She holds beginner, Spreadsheet Sheila's hand and step by step, she shows her what it takes and what to do to learn now to use Excel formulas and functions.

Her everyday language and brilliant metaphors, illustrate her points clearly.

The links to relevant resources needed for you to practice what Sheila is learning, plus the tools are there, just where needed.

In easy to follow stages Anne walks her through everything she needs to get good at Excel.   With nothing left to chance, piece by piece you too can get to grips with how to use Excel. It's like a detective novel and you end up solving the case!

Ann Kelly,
Personal Development coach/owner
- Reaching Your Potential

www.ingramcontent.com/pod-product-compliance
Lightning Source LLC
LaVergne TN
LVHW012335060326
832902LV00012B/1901